DON'T
LET THE
DAFFODILS
FOOL YOU

DON'T LET THE DAFFODILS FOOL YOU

A Collection of Poetry
and Spoken Word

PJ

PHOENIX JAMES

DON'T LET THE DAFFODILS FOOL YOU

First Edition: 2022

ISBN: 978-1-7397925-4-1 (Paperback)
ISBN: 978-1-7397925-5-8 (Ebook)

Cover Artwork & Design by Phoenix James.
Book Design & Formatting by Phoenix James.

Visit the author's website at www.PhoenixJamesOfficial.com or email him at phoenix@PhoenixJamesOfficial.com

DEDICATION

To all who did
To all who couldn't
To all who can
To all who will
And to all who do
I hope this adds something

And to a young boy
Who a long time ago
Guided only by faith
And relentless tenacity
Took great courage
And went his own way

Thank you for your guidance
For your strength of character
Your persistent determination
And your unwavering perseverance
You are the reason I am here

I hope I've honoured your efforts
And made your journey worthwhile.

CONTENTS

ALL THAT IS GREAT

I wish you well
I wish you good health
I wish you clarity
I wish you guidance
I wish you mentorship
In some way
Shape or form
In whatever way that comes

Mentorship
Can come through many ways
Not just counselling
With another human being
It can come through
The type of music you listen to
It can come through friends
It can come through family
It can come through art
And creativity
It can come through
Listening to motivational material
I wish you mentorship
In some way shape or form
That inspires you

I wish you positivity
I wish you progress
I wish you
Clear perspective
On your goals
Ambitions
Desires

I wish you clarity
I do wish you clarity
I wish you clear vision
I wish you strength
I wish you courage

I wish you wouldn't worry
And concern yourself
With the opinions of others
I wish you resilience
I wish you distance
From the things
That no longer serve you
No longer add to you
No longer uplift you

I wish you direction
I wish you self-assuredness

I wish you self confidence
I wish you the ability
To self assess you

Aside from
And amidst the voices
The external voices
That we often allow
To get inside
That we internalise

You're not good enough
Why are you doing this
Do you think
You're going to succeed
Why don't you
Stick to what you're good at

I wish you peace
I wish you prosperity
I wish you an abundance
Of good things

I wish you wholeness
I wish you completeness
I wish you fulfilment

I wish you a place
Where it is safe
To lean
On your own understanding

I wish you discernment
I wish you knowledge of self
I wish you knowledge of others
I wish you an understanding
Of thoughts
Of your own
And the thoughts
Of others around you

I wish you awareness
I wish you most of all
Patience
Patience to know
That all good things
Come to those who work
And that all good things
Require time
And energy
And fuel

I wish you life

I wish you love
I wish you happiness
I wish you foresight
I wish you fortitude
And I wish you faith
I wish you all that is good
And all that is great.

ALL USED UP

I hope you
Save or hold nothing back
Of yourself in this life
I hope you learn to let go
Let go until your heart
And your palms are light
And bare
Until you free your feet
And give birth to wings
Until your mind and spirit
Find peace
I hope you lay it all out
All of it
Everything
Everything you came with
Everything you now have
All you collected
And accumulated
Learned and gathered
And became attached
To carrying with you
Along your way
Those treasures
You forgot you had

Buried somewhere inside
I hope you discover them again
One day
When something feels absent
And you're not sure where you are
I hope you leave them all here
Your light and your dark places
All that you are
All that you were
And have to give now
Leave them behind
For others to find
Here where our gifts
Are only given to us
To be given away
Just like your brilliant smile
It is of no worth to you
Until it is presented
To another
Here
Where you are of most use
As was intended
Here
Where light begets light
And chases away shadows
By the time your wings

Take you beyond this place
I hope you have left
Nothing of your self
I hope you take nothing
Of your value with you
That you leave
Each and every one
Of your special little
Precious gems behind
That your soul floats lightly
In the knowing
That you gave
Much more than you took
I hope you rise
Filled abundantly
With all life gave you
But yet satisfyingly empty
Not a thing unseen
Unshared
Unsaid
Undiscovered
Or undone
When you leave
May it be with an empty cup
By such time
I hope you're all used up.

ALL WE HAVE

We chase and we chase
We want it all now
Too often
At the sacrifice
Of the things
That really matter
The things that won't wait
The things we need
Most of all
While we madly pursue
The things that will keep
The opportunities
The endeavours
That we feel
May be slipping
Through our fingers
Losing our grasp
Trying to hold onto things
Things
That change form and fashion
As quickly as we do
The wants we finally receive
Become the things
We no longer desire

We've let go
To chase after new ones
The chances
That always
Come around again
Losing sight
Of the moments that won't
It doesn't all have to be now
Because what's most important
Is that now
Is all we have.

BLUE SUNSHINE

Whatever you do
Whatever you go through
Always got to remember
That someone
Has got it worse than you

Please
You're complaining it's raining
But you haven't ever seen the day
When you had to pray for rain
Just so you could get something
To drink again
And something to eat

Oh
You cut open your leg?
That's sweet
I know a man
Who stepped
On the wrong train one day
Now he's an amputee
See
We each need
To walk in the thought

That someone somewhere
Has got it worse off than me

You and your neighbour got beef?
Oh please
How about if you
Went to the shop one week
To get your meat
And found out
All you really got
Was mad cow disease

Somebody crashed into your car?
Oh but, you're still living though, right?
Well how about
Going to your family's funeral
Because some guy
Thought it was cool
To drink and drive
Or maybe your own funeral
Since you're so unhappy
About your life

Lost your job?
Damn
Guess things are completely

Over for you, man
There'll never be another
Looks like all you can do now
Is weep
And eat out of garbage cans
And watch everything you've learnt
Just wither away in your hands
Hey
Does that sound like a plan?
After all
Everything you've got going on
Is just so bad

What?
Are you mad
Because someone
Just stepped on your new shoes
Well
What you are you going to do?
How about
We hand them to the man
Who never had any shoes
Or maybe
We should take them
Back to the sweatshop
Where some kid

Gets not a lot to make them
Working his fingertips to the bone
But can't afford to take a trip
To see the success of his creation
So know that you're not alone
And that somebody
Has always
Got it worse than you
No matter what you're facing.

DON'T

Don't view me as a tyrant
Due to the things I say
Don't do the things
That I don't like
And we just might be okay
Don't offer me your cigarettes
Don't offer me your beers
Don't offer me a lifestyle
That only leads to tears
Don't offer me your chronic
Don't offer me your weed
Don't offer me any substances
My body doesn't need
Don't offer me dead flesh
From a dead carcass
Whether chicken breast
Pork
Or red meat
Don't offer me poison
And then expect me to eat
Don't tell me that you love me
When really you don't care
Don't say you've got my back
When you're hardly there

Don't say that I can count on you
Whenever I feel myself
Falling out the frame
Don't talk about the amount
Of times you let me down
Don't let me start
Calling out your name
Don't be smiling
When you see me
And then be talking
Behind my back
Because you know
That's out of place
Don't ever let it get back to me
Because I just might
Punch you in your face
Don't consider me violent
Just speaking out on how I feel
If I just stayed silent
Then I wouldn't be being real
Don't tell me I should sing
Baby, why don't you
If I wanted to sing, my love
Then that's what I would do
Don't lie or twist my words
And we'll all be cool

Don't try to diss my girl
That's a world for fools
Don't tell me how I'm living
How it is
And how it isn't
Don't give me a religion
Designed
To keep my mind imprisoned
Don't tell me that I'm lost
And that I should be saved
There will be no
Saving me for later
That's how the devil gets his way
Don't quote me your philosophies
That really make no sense at all
Why should a man
Turn the other cheek
When his back is against the wall
Don't teach me his histories
Teach me mine
So I can shine in my glory
Don't preach to me the mysteries
That time can't define for me
Don't kill my brother
My brother, you forget
One day I hope you'll remember

You say you wouldn't join the KKK
But yet you act like a member
Don't talk with me
If you're saying
You aren't really ready
To take it to the top
Don't walk with me
If along the way
You know you might stop
Don't view me as a tyrant
Due to the things I say
Don't do the things that I don't like
And maybe
Just maybe we might be okay.

DRESSING UP FOR A FIRST DATE

I remembered
Having a date one time
That day
I felt I'd really dress up
And look great
Making that extra effort
In my appearance
For no reason at all
It's just the mood I was in
It just so happens
I had the date that afternoon too
It made her uncomfortable
She couldn't comprehend
Why I was so dressed up
She asked a couple of times
If I was going to church afterwards
I told her it was just my mood
And how I was feeling that day
I could tell she wasn't content
With that as my reason
For being so dressed up
What I thought would impress her
Unnerved her instead
The conversation

About my attire
Was just one of a few factors
That for me
Made the whole experience
Unfavourable
Overall
It was truly the most awkward
And uncomfortable date
I've ever been on
That was the one
And only time we met
And haven't been in touch
With each other
Since that day
It crossed my mind today
For some reason.

DRINK DRIVE, THINK TWICE

After work last week
I decided to get behind the wheel
Even though I'd been drinking again
Didn't think anything of it
Used to think it was all a big joke
But I guess that was then
It still seems like only last night
That we were finishing up the displays
And just getting ready to leave
John said
He was going past the station that day
So I gave him a lift
With Pat and Steve
He said he had to pick up some tickets
For the show on Monday evening
For him and his wife
He said the couple from next door
Went the week before
And said it was really nice
I remember us deciding to stop off
At our usual place for a drink
Before we all went home
As we came in
It was a surprise to see Paul

In the corner by himself
Drinking alone
Apparently him and his wife
Had a serious argument
And she threw him out
With all his stuff
He was so upset
We must have spent about at least
An hour and a half or more
Trying to cheer him up
After chatting over a game of pool
For what must have been
At least another hour or so
We had a few more drinks
And then decided to go
John had been trying to give up drinking
And was so pleased with the fact
That he didn't drink any alcohol
And that he managed to stay sober
He started to tell us a story
About the last time he drank
And drove his car
And the police had to pull him over
For a second he made me think
And wonder if that was meant to be
Some kind of sign or warning to me

Or not
But by the time
We made it to the car
And got inside
I had totally forgot
I was just about to pull out
When Paul jumped forward in his seat
And suggested
That since we'd all been drinking
Maybe John should drive the car
But I myself
Didn't really see the need
I was fine
And plus it wasn't really that far
They started arguing with me
So I said if they didn't like it
They should get out and walk
And that they were acting like kids
I didn't really expect
That they would seriously go
But one by one they did
I didn't really care at the time
I was too angry to call them back
I'm very stubborn in that way
Once I've spoken, that's that
I drove off

And turned left onto the main road
That would take me home
I remember thinking nothing of it
But at the time
Who would have known
Now I really wish I'd listened
To all those crazy warnings
On the posters
And on the TV
They used to advertise
Back then
I never really took it seriously
Never really thought twice
I can still hear
Paul and Steve's words
Warning me
Telling me I'm not up to it
And that I really shouldn't drive
Maybe if I'd listened
Maybe if I'd taken heed
Maybe I'd still be alive.

DROWNING WORLD

Days and nights are cold
The corners are hot
Gunshots ringing off
On the block
Kids can't sleep
And it never stops
It's either the sirens
Or the shots
Another dead
Some seek peace
Within the hip-hop
Keep your feet to the beat
Pressing on
Keep your feet to the street
Knowing some
Won't make it home tonight
That's our life
We were all born
Into a drowning world
Will we die?
What's the future
For our boys and girls?
Will we survive?
Through the unification

Of our bodies
Spirits and minds
Overcoming this oppression
Overpowering our lives
Hard faces
Hard places
And hard times
Through our passion
And these words
Still we rise
Still we rise.

ENOUGH SAID

As much as we suppose
No one actually knows
What the future holds
Except that it's somewhere
We each and all have to go
I've been setting new targets
Bigger goals
Making new plans
Resculpting and remoulding
An old artist
Into a new man
It starts to get rewarding
Telling yourself you can
I'm changing
Though I look the same
I hope you understand

It's still all about progression
Live and let live
I guess it is what it is
I've learned my lesson
No longer focused on what isn't
And what could've been
It's too depressing

Just focused on the mission
And the message
Listening to everything
My soul is expressing
Letting go of all of this regret
And this aggression
Because looking forward
There's way too many blessings
Easier said than done
These times are testing
But you should do the same too
Is my suggestion

They'll enquire where you are
When you're not in town
Then ask who are you
When you're back around
Don't worry he didn't die
I'm still living
Still flying
Still firing
It didn't kill him
What makes you stronger
Should also make you meek
One day you're here
Then may be gone in a week

What you say and do not say
Can take you to the peak
Needless to say
With what you do say
Watch the way you speak

You'll say a thing
Nothing that hasn't been said before
But you'll say it in such a way
That resonates
And they'll want to
Hear you say some more
So much is said
So much unsaid
All so many things
What not to forget
Is that peace and freedom
Begins only from within
With all that said
With all that is said
I hope you say too much
Who wants to be dead
And didn't say enough.

ENSLAVED

Shackled
In chains that bind me
From head to toe
I ponder on why
I have been brought
To this position
To be beaten
And dragged
From my own homeland
Against my own permission
I had a house and land
A wife and three sons
And of all of this
Now I have none
I pray for the pain to go away
But as I pray
Only more comes
I had a new born baby girl
That I've only seen twice
I cry as I wonder
What will become of her life
If torn away from her mother
How could she possibly survive
We mean nothing

To these people
Who have come
In every way but peace
I can see it in their actions
As my brother pleas for his release
I still have strong faith
Even though
My freedom of movement
And freedom of choice
Now seem a thing of the past
I still have my thoughts
But how long will they last
These are my only vices now
And the things that keep me
From going insane
My thoughts of my past
Are the healers of my pain
These strangers
Have come from other shores
And speak a language
That to us is unknown
So some of us
Just stare in silence
While some of us
Scream for home
And because they shout

Violent angry words
Of which we do not understand
We cannot respond
So they use their hands
To beat us down
Drawing blood as they see fit
Death is the result of lives
Who choose not to submit
Who gives these people the right
To invade our land
And enslave us
Against our will
Who gives them the authority
To have my brother killed
Such wickedness is this
That I see before my face
Pregnant mothers stripped
And beaten
To shame and disgrace
These bloody scenes
I know will stay with me
For the remainder of my days
I know I'll forever see the faces
Of those whom I couldn't save
But just as my persecutors
Lash out

And strike me once more
I realise a fear in their eyes
I had never seen before
And as the blood
Runs down my forehead
Into my face
I find
These people
Can restrain my body
But never my mind.

GLORY DAY

Their spirit
Constantly serves to remind me
She is coming
So I keep myself here
Always in preparation
For her arrival
These ancient men say
She passes your way
Only but once
So I continue pressing on
I wish to be ready
When she comes
And when she does
I will not be afraid
I will go
Peacefully along her way
I pray
She will accept my humble efforts
And see them as worthy
Of her presence
I yearn for her acceptance
This I long for everyday
And a shooting star
Still confirms my birthright

Over a million miles away
And I am here
With the love of angels
Within my circumference
So why should I fear
Here where the rhythm of silence
Now is as beautiful
As when I speak
These wonders
I have been told in whispers
In stares
And gestures
Breaths of hope
Here where my full moon
Is so much fuller now
Means so much more now
Again
The sky never lapses
Still paints pictures that say
This is what men of honour quest for
These are what the stones
Of the builder look like
This is the colour
Of the bricks on the road
This way leads to your fortress
And this is where the fork is

Beware
Time is friend or foe
Always
Though you decide
Which way the spoon bends
And when
Outside of your hands
Is how soon it ends
Always
And I adore the message
This landscape conveys
It shines more beautiful
And says more
Than I could ever hope to portray
And that's okay
I know my place
And that she is coming for me
Like the men of old say
I know her face
I see her in my dreams everyday
I will welcome her
With all and everything inside me
That desires her more
Than any living thing
She's worth dying for
My beautiful children

Will know me best
Through her
And because my overbearing
Determination
Has and will always
Continue to drive me
In pursuit of her
They will be blessed
And highly favoured
And remembered
In life
And even in death
As will their father
And their children
I will carry this
And bear it forever
Until she comes for me
And I will go peacefully
And freely
As if it were merely death
Softly calling me
Rather than glory
My day cometh
And I live for it
This is my story.

GOD HELP THE OUTCAST

God help the outcasts
Not to lose their way
In you may they find refuge
This very day
Forlorn in a world
Where good hearts
Seem few and far between
Let them understand
Their way is supreme
Ordained by you
To be the fishers of men
To lead the gone astray
Back to you again
Often ridiculed
Because they speak
Of righteous things
Let the words of the unwise
Be as the soft blowing winds
Never strong enough
To uproot
The trees of life
Planted in you
Never strong enough
For a righteous mans heart

To be moved
For he and all those like him
Always suffer condemnation
Once your name
Is the topic
Of our conversation.

I.S.O.P.O.T.E.O.T.E.P

As I awoke
From the floor
Of the inside
Of a speeding black cab
From all the drugs they gave me
In order to sedate me
I managed to rise to my knees
And bang on the glass
Asking
Who are you
And where are you taking me
But the mysterious driver
Continued to tear through
The dark wet streets
As if oblivious
Not turning to face me
Suddenly it struck me
This was one of the three
Who had chased me
I was foolish
Not to consider
That knowledge
Of the Estrangement Papers
Could place me in danger

Or that I should have
Concealed my identity
From Mission Alpha
And remained a stranger
But it never seemed overly risky
For me to diffuse knowledge
Of the parchments
And their information myself
Via the Phenzology dialogues
But how wrong I was
Now I know undoubtedly
There are charlatans
Moving in on the entire case
And unhesitant to use violence
From Zimbabwe to Germany
Back to London
And I'm still not safe
They operate
In subliminal silence
Watching my every move
Trying to elicit responses
But I just stay wise
And keep quiet
Until more can be proved
Unexpectedly the bell sounds
And there's a familiar

But impatient
Knocking at the door
I head to the staircase
The hallway clock says 7:44
It was F6
Back from his flight to Vancouver
A little sooner than expected
On entering
He said
I had to see you
We have to regroup and re-route
Our agents in Russia
Have contacted us
With news of a new breakthrough
We reached the top of the staircase
And walked back across the hallway
To my room
He continued
With all our research
Into the E.P.O
It can now be proven and shown
That Mission Alpha
Sent out an earth probe
Designed to watch and observe
Every soul on the entire globe
Which we were told

Even in its subordinate mode
Was so powerful
That from space
It could read the information
From a coin in the road
These technological capabilities
Are being incorporated
To monitor calls
On mobile phones
But that's not all
They also talked about
The fibre optic frequencies
Running through TV's
With the ability
To transmit and receive
Which means
That when you think
You're watching BBC2
BBC2 is watching you
But whilst still in search of proof
Of the existence
Of the Estrangement Papers
There's not much we can do
Without endangering our lives too
He paused
Then said

But in time
The world will have to face it
That this matrix
Was designed
To keep our minds castrated
Created to keep us blind
And that there are no more
Safe places to hide
Once you've discovered
And uncovered the signs
That reside inside the sacred papers
Estrange means divide
Which explains why
They've always tried
To separate us
And make us
Hate us
Suddenly
There's a loud bang downstairs
And a huge commotion as they broke in
I instantly read the situation
Somehow Mission Alpha
Must have been informed
Of the operation
And sent out their Agents
To follow F6

Which obviously
Led to my location
We had to move fast
The Agents
Were sent with one task
To kill us both
No hesitation
Or questions asked
I know now that conversations
Of the Estrangement Papers
In the wrong places
Is walking a dangerous path
Trusting the wrong faces
And trusting the wrong people
In the past
Has led me to this
Running away
Down a dark alleyway
With my heart
Beating fast
As they chase me
I parted from F6
It was for our own safety
And as they keep chasing
And chasing
And I keep running

And running
It's becoming obvious
That they weren't sent to kill us
As I had thought
Back at the location
But just for our capture
And to bring us back
To Mission Alpha
Because they knew
We had information
And as I awoke
From the floor
Of the inside
Of a speeding black cab
From all the drugs they gave me
In order to sedate me
I managed to rise to my knees
And bang on the glass
Asking
Who are you
And where are you taking me
But the mysterious driver
Continued to tear through
The dark wet streets
As if oblivious
Not turning to face me

Suddenly it struck me
This was one of the three
Who had chased me.

IN THE PROCESS

The edit
Just wasn't working
I had to go back in
Take it apart
And start from scratch
At the very beginning
Shot by shot
I had to separate the *necessary* shots
From the, what I call
The *nice to have* shots
A process of elimination
Where many of the *nice to haves*
Would be no more
I extended the length
Of the *necessary* shots
To meet the length
Of the overall narrative
Of the piece
It worked very well
In fact it worked much better
Than my initial vision
Of what the final piece
Would ultimately be
It became a smoother

Tighter
More succinct work
Another one of those
More often than not
Cases where
Less is more
Sometimes it just goes that way
Within the creative process
Things change
From how you originally
Envisioned the final look
Sound or feel
Of the thing you're creating
The piece itself
Always tells you
What it's meant to be
And takes you in that direction
If you're willing to listen
And be guided
By the creative energy
You've tuned into
Which is to be open
At all times while creating
Allowing yourself
To be lead
By the same energy

That brought it all to you
In the first place
It can be considered
A give and take relationship
With your self
And creative energy
A collaborative endeavour
A tuning in
An exchange
A conversation
Between you
As the earth
And the greater
Surrounding universe.

INAUGURAL CELEBRATION

We come
From another place
And another time
A place
Where time
Has no place
We are the voices
Of the future
Present
And past
We are yesterday's
Cosmic spirits
And tomorrow's people
We are words
Sounds
And power
Our words
And sounds
Are energy
And have the power
To create change
We are the writers
Wordsmiths
Lyricists

Poets
Modern-day scribes
Griots
Messengers
Thinkers
Visionaries
Bringers forth
Of prophecy
The foretellers
Of the foretold
Documenters
Of the old
And new world
We have no roots
In any organised religion
But all religion
Has its roots in us
Our purpose
Our names
And their meanings
Have been
And shall be
Etched into
And engraved
On walls
And in the minds

Of our children
And their children
And their children's children
We are before
And shall be after
We are sent
And shall send others
There are many of us
And shall be many more
With many directions
And many aims
But among us
One common cause
Join us
In celebration
And remembrance
Of this
That shall never
Pass away
But live
Forever.

INVOCATION

You stayed and prayed
By my grave for days
Sang songs of praise for me
Played CDs
And tapes of me
Brought water
From the sacred lake
And sat by the fire place for me
Telling my stories
Waiting patiently
Hoping
It would all awaken me
Peacefully
That I would not rest
For eternity
But rise and return to thee
Eternally
And that those
Who sought my demise
Would be forgiven
Thank you
For bringing me back
For now
I have risen.

LOVE & PHOTOSYNTHESIS

Love the universe
Love the cycles of the earth
Life is purer than water
Love the rainforest
What's left
And all that it's worth
Love the roots of nature
Love spiritual development
Of non-progressive elements
Be not a partaker
Love not money
Not necessary like oxygen
The two are not equal
Love knowledge
Love wisdom
But most of all
Love people

Our relationships of today
Steer more and more
Away from sharing
It's like the way in which
The steering wheel of a car
In a right turn

Steers away from the gearing
Birth control pills
Produce nil
Destructive
And non-productive
Like a human
With only the will to kill
We were once
Drawn together
In a process
Complex like photosynthesis
But now
The chemicals
Of a now polluted atmosphere
Have counteracted here all of this
Nothing remains natural
As once upon a time
Not the air
Not our hair
Not even the fruits upon the tree
For they too are infected
Before their gestation
Much like the truth is neglected
Making way for the lies
That spread far and wide
Like the sickness of radiation

Love the universe
Love the cycles of the earth
Life is purer than water
Love the rainforest
What's left
And all that it's worth
Love the roots of nature
Love spiritual development
Of non-progressive elements
Be not a partaker
Love not money
Not necessary like oxygen
The two are not equal
Love knowledge
Love wisdom
But most of all
Love people.

MINDLESS TIME vs. TIMELESS MIND

I am the creator
Of the preceding
And the bygone

I see the future
From afar
And beyond

Way down yonder
I see it
And I see
That time is running out

But my time
Is beyond
The tick tock tick

For I sail
On metaphoric time ships
Designed to make minds flip
I climb the highest heights
Whilst I just
Sit

When time first spotted me
It made a dash to stop me
But all it did was trip

And by the time
I finish this rhyme
Some will comprehend
While for others
It just didn't
Click.

MINNEAPOLIS BURNING

There's rioting
Violence
And protesting
In the streets
An unarmed black man
Dead
Couldn't breathe
Life snatched
At the hands of crooked police
The definition of excessive force
Broadcasts
As the world sees
However
The root cause of the unrest
Is seldom appeased
But regardless
Is surely always followed
By mention of peace
Tensions increase
Beyond the harsh rattle of bullets
Batons
And tear gas
As the National Guard
Is tasked to respond

In battle
To fight them back
The deafening
Angry noises
Of grievance
Won't be easily silenced
By more needless violence
To achieve compliance
Watch live another life taken
Just add it to the quota
Of those long gone
And those
Who still long for closure
Many won't sleep tonight
In Minneapolis, Minnesota
It will be a long time
Before all of this is over
As we mourn one more
Of life's black murdered soldiers
Police just killed
A restrained
And incapacitated George Floyd
Out in public view
We all got to watch
Up-close
Without a thing we could do

I wasn't there
But I read about it everywhere
And saw it in the news
"I can't breathe"
Imagine it was me
Imagine it was me standing
Watching you
Laying breathless
And helpless
Unable to change your fate
Pleading with the officers
Who had you pinned down
Before it became too late
Graphic imagery
Of a white police officer
Kneeling his weight
On a black man's neck
Who was already cuffed
Face down
On the ground
So why that was necessary
I'll never get
Nevertheless
I hear that he called out
To his late mother
With his last breath

And that a paramedic
On the scene
Was refused permission
To do a pulse check
I've heard
Police officers can't refuse that
But I don't know enough yet
So much is done
So much is unsaid
So much is truth
Yet mostly incorrect
Being black
Shouldn't be a death sentence
I heard the Mayor say
And I read
George's mother passed
Two years ago to the day
I hope they'll meet
Again together
Somewhere along the way
The people
Won't be sleeping peacefully
In Minneapolis
Someone will have to pay
The city's streets
Are burning

As the acts of authority
Come under fire
Until justice is served
They'll just keep justifying the riots
The people just want to be heard
The people are just tired
It's not enough
Whenever murdering cops
Are just fired
First priority
Is the preservation of life
Says the Chief of police
And there the blinding irony lies
Way beyond belief
While the FBI
And Attorneys office request
For people's patience
And more information
To help assist
In their investigation
To determine whether
A crime has been committed
The people's frustration decides
They've already seen
All the evidence they need
Therefore

That time is not permitted
Meanwhile
Two black members
Of the CNN press
Reporting live on the protests
Were placed under arrest
I say it in jest
But on this day
Police say
Freedom of journalism
Will not be televised I guess
Yet the cameras
Keep on recording
And the internet
Keeps on reporting
Reposting
Forwarding
Rehashing
Tagging
And retweeting
Taking action
On these new platforms
For speaking
Sharing
In this new modern era
Of reaching

There once was a time
I used to refuse to look
And instead chose to hide
From the emotions I felt
From the brutality I saw
That hurt me inside
But I've heard and learned
That the poet
Must not overt his eyes
Especially from the cruel sight
Of injustices
And the images of lies
Deep down
It's all too familiar
And doesn't come as any surprise
We've seen and heard
This inconceivable narrative
Play out so many countless times
Witness another
Unbelievable police snuff film
See the evil of another
Innocent black man killed
What is it that compels someone
To put his knee into a man's neck
And hold it there
Until that man

Can no longer draw breath
Actions of a man
Sworn in to preserve life
As well as to serve and protect
None in Minneapolis will sleep easy
Amidst this period
Of civil unrest
For what satisfactory justice
Does a wrongfully
Murdered
Black man get.

For George Floyd
Unlawfully murdered by Police in
Minneapolis, Minnesota, United States on
Monday 25th May 2020.

And all of the countless numbers of others
everywhere who unjustly lost their lives at
the hands of law enforcement.

For all those who speak for them in their
absence.

MY DR. MARTENS

I own a pair of boots
A pair of Dr. Martens
Yeah I do
And every time I wear them
I feel so brand new
Elated by
And hooked on
Their ability
To make me
Look better than you
Yes
Ego gets a real boost
But not just any old pair of shoes
Mind you
Been around since 1960
And they still shine too
Still top of the line too
When I'm in my DM's
I'm pleased
These are the D's
In it's been a DM good day
The M's in much more manageable
Than blue suede
My top of the range

Goodyear Welted construction
And heat sealed soles
Are designed
So my feet won't see holes
I won't feel cold
In my Performance Leather
Like those with their toes
Exposed in cold weather
My EVA filler
With Bouncing Soles
Give me so much pleasure
At work or at leisure
My DM's
Can make me smart
Smooth
Rude
Cool
Or clever
I treat them like a baby
Taking the utmost coochy-coo care
Had the Gucci shoe
Even had the Nike Air
But nothing can compare
To my Dr. Martens AirWair.

NO RETREAT, NO SURRENDER

Why just recite poetry
When I can turn words
To sodium nitrate
Ignite each verse
Watch it explode
And feel my soul vibrate
Shaking demons off
Propelling me closer
To my dreams and goals
And the achievement of
It's expensive
Keeping the flame alight though
You wouldn't believe the cost
Sacrifice
Sometimes
You have to die to be alive
So I don't grieve the loss
And as long as
I can still taste
The sulphur on my lips
I know I can burn every vulture
Off that cliff
And what can you tell me
Nothing

Until you know what it is
To be down in that valley
Surrounded
Praying
That the fables aren't true
But praying to who
They say god left this place
Long before you were born
So that leaves them
And you
In a dusty torn robe
Grazed elbows
And dirty finger nails
From scratching at the stones
Trying to escape
To some other place
Doesn't matter
Just somewhere else
We create our world
And try to escape from our self
Tripping over
At every attempt
As though our feet were tied
Falling to our knees
Crying to the skies
Begging for time

To slow down
So we can
Catch a piece of the sun
Before it disappears
Behind the horizon
And now
That your time has come
Have no regrets

Except
That you couldn't
Tell somebody sooner

That when the solar rays
That radiate their day
Fade away
That they could use the moonlight
To illuminate their night
Just as bright
That no condition
Is permanent
And that it's okay to cry
That even the wise
Are still learning
And that in every wrong
There's a right

I don't care
If you have to lay booby traps
And tripwire
Through the forest

Plant letter bombs
In their mailboxes

Wire live grenades
To their doorframes

Detonate dynamite
Under their cars

Desecrate their places of worship

Set fire to their gods

Use violence
Use politics
Use sex
Use science

Peace keep with guns
Drop bombs
And demand silence

Get them
Demand their attention
And when they're listening
Tell them

The only thing consistent
Is change
And therefore
Things are only permanent

Temporarily.

OF A BROKEN WORLD

I think we're all broken
Before we get here
We are born
Of broken people
Who too
Were born of broken people
As were those before them
We are all products
Of a broken world
A breaking planet
With a nature
To give birth to things
Only to watch them die
Like a wilting flower
A dying fruit
A fallen tree
A decaying building
An eroding coastline
A fading sunset
We are no exception
There is nothing held onto
That subconscious
Realisation
In itself

Breaks you
Those who live
Under the illusion
That we aren't inherently
Born broken
Break the most
Life is a journey
Spent finding
Putting
Or keeping
All of our little
Broken pieces
Of ourselves
Together
For as long as we can.

POET'S PAVILION

Let me set the scene
It was 10.15
Below the first floor
Of the Theatre Bar
Cars
Were just pulling up outside
And so was ours
Club Phoenix
Was blazing
A little further on
Down the street
But I never went there
It just wasn't for me
Don't do drugs
Don't drink
And I'm straight
Don't gamble
Don't play
Committed to the spirit now
So I just mingle
Like a man not single
Definitely not my kind of place
In fact
None of ours

We preferred jazz cafes
And wine bars
Where the essence
Of spoken word
Could be heard
Part of the blessings
After a hard days work
To be able to receive
Those healing melodies
Relaxed by candle light
With rest for tired feet
To be uplifted
And soothed
By the calming
Of spiritually rhythmic beat
The aromatic fragrance
Of incense
Smells sweet
As it flows out
From the Poet's Pavilion
Into the street
And I'm thinking
Now that's where
I'd rather be.

SOLDIER SONG

Lately
I've been meditating
And whispering
Walking through Memphis
And Saqqarah
Listening for shooting stars
Leaving footprints
In the Sahara
Discretely
Etching my name
On tombstones
And shrines
Collecting chippings
Of limestone
And old bones
Trying to communicate
With the dead
In attempts
To reclaim my eternity
So that you and I
Will never die
But live forever
Permanently
And eternally

Yes
This
Restless
Never surrender soldier
Whose battle won't be over
Until he passes over
So stop trying to define me
Just get behind me
Send word to others
And tell them that they'll find me
On my knees
In Karnak
Washing my face
In the Sacred Lake
Trying to receive blessings
For my journey back
Back through the crossroads
Been on this planet thirty times
And I've still got to think hard
Which way to go
So don't disturb me
I'm busy
Otherwise engaged
Trying to stay connected
Been mastering phonetics
And channelling spirits

Mixed with neurolinguistics
So that when I spit these lyrics
They stick
Creating road maps
To redirect a troubled soul
And I feel like time is short
So don't waste it
Asking me my goal
I have no point to be reached
No specific plan
Just understand
That for my futures
I've been breathing
Into microphones
Relishing the feeling
Of being home
And I'm not far now
Just got to keep creative
Stay focused
And remain blessed
See
A woman told me
She's been reading my poetry
To her kids at night
And in that light
That's more than enough reason

For me to live this life
Push on through soldier
Keep doing your thing
Whenever I come marching through
That's the song the crowd sing
And I surely will
But at the same time
I wonder if they're aware
Of the prices paid to be here
The sacrifices made
To steer clear of pain
And if my enemies realise
It's a blessing
Whenever they mention my name
As my immortality
Dances on the tips of their tongues
And their brains
I can assure you
What was meant to be here
Will never change
So dissect me
Disbeliever
Separate me and see
You'll just be creating
Another way for me to be free
I'm not walking this road alone

No
Take my life
Or let me go
I'll still be going home
Take all I own
But look into my eyes
And know that it is known
My mirror reflects God
And the footsteps of martyrs
And that my make-up
Was designed to take me up
Whenever the going gets harder
You will forget me not
Standing
On the rocks of the harbour
Arms stretched out
Across the wild ocean
In devotion
My skin
Absorbing the sea spray
Of my ancestors essence
Like magic potion
I receive now
My aura
Weighing heavy
Overbearing

And deep-rooted
Like old oak trees
No need to question
Whether I've been here before
Please
See that these lines
Are more than metaphors
And these minds
With closed doors
Will open
In due course
Singing this same soldier's melody
Coming forth
Holding its energy
Remember me
And send for me
Via the source
Bring me my sword
And my horse
Endlessly
A union
Without divorce
Replenish me.

STEP FORWARD

Hey, you
Yes, you
Standing on the wall
There's a cultural revolution going on
And this is the final call
Those who are taking part
Might want to Step Forward some more
So that those who are not
Can make their way out quietly
By the door
But don't Step Forward
If for some reason
You feel you're unsure
Because we need
Strong men and women
Who aren't afraid of war
Strong men and women
Who are prepared to fight
For the cause
Things could indeed break out
At any moment
That's why we need warriors
That's why we need soldiers
Male and female

Armed with lyrical fitness
And diction
Please do not Step Forward
If you do not fit this description
Hey, you
Yes, you lot
Standing by the bar
There's a cultural revolution going on
And you're way too far
You might want to Step Forward
And claim your position
Or just simply listen
To find out whether or not
You're fit for the mission
I say whether
Rapper
Singer
Poet
Or MC
Within this cultural revolution
Is where you need to be
Step Forward.

STRANGELAND

I felt strong as an oxen
When I had my locks 'n
A life in the sun
Without shoes 'n socks 'n
Sometimes sandals
But mostly bare feet on the beach
No Reeboks n' no Docs n'
Skin was clear
No late night greasy feast
To give me spots n'
Fresh fruit n' veg
Without the toxins
Thanks a lot
For your
Chemically processed things
Now I feel myself in need
For detoxin'
In a strange land
Where they
Minimised my options
For health
I laugh to myself
While Radoxin'
In the bath

Thinking
Look at this crazy mess
They got us in
I'm listening to Coxen
Sound system
Blaring out from the kitchen
Reminiscing
On when things were different
How things have changed
Are things still the same
They most definitely isn't
Used to be a free man
Now I'm living
In a strange land prison
With an exception for my mind
Won't be conditioned
Without permission
In a life and times
Of ism schism
I find
It's a terrible crime
To be different
Or to want the choice
To make my own decisions
This ain't living
I want to be free

From this strange land
Please take me
By the hand
For the things
I've become accustomed to
Have made me
Less than a man
From this strange
Strangeland
Please return me
To who I am.

THE ANCESTOR'S SONG

The ancestors
Sing a song
From within the ink
That flows from my pen
They sing and they sing
And closer and closer
I push it to them
Penning out their
Aggravations
And their
Pent-up frustration
They sing I must take my station
And trust their administration
I am prescribed
As the required medication
And I must be willing
To accept my delegation
As the powerful penicillin
Devised to combat the pathogens
Infecting this nation
That I must give praise
And appreciation
That I am not the worst
Neither the last

Nor first
But the penultimate
Sent to quench
Man's insipid verse
So that today's
Awakening slaves
May not thirst
But open their eyes
To realise
The plight of their curse
And that there's no price on earth
To match their worth
They need to rise from the dirt
And recognise
That we worked
So hard
So you all could be here today
They say
We are an ungrateful disgrace
We forsake the sacrifice
They made for our life
We're displaced
And suffer from a serious case
Of conceptual incarceration
They say they won't let me rest
Until I express

Their indignation
In my conversation
Anytime I bless the mic
Or take the stage
At these occasions
So I bear no resistance
To their pentatonic scales
That continually
Haunt my existence
And never fail
To bring me back
To the land of the living
When I am slipping
Singing
Do not give in
Do not give in
That I am born
As one of their
Shining stars of hope
That amidst the thorns
I will be the rose
That never chokes
But continually grows
As long as I never relinquish
My position
Within this mission

For which I'm chose
And remember
That my grandmother said
No fret
The holes in her dress
Could never compare
To the holes
Branded
Into our ancestors flesh
Though now we compare that
To the holes
Blown
Into another brother's chest
For less than you'd expect
From a race established
In honour
And respect
Nevertheless
Never forget
The quest we have set
For it is already said
There will be
Victims of their victims
And victims of their test
And there will only be
Reconciliation

When we
Can finally
Rest.

THE GAME OF LIFE II

Not quite a party song
But just another song
To keep my party strong
And keep them moving on
Because it won't be long
I'm trying to build my team
And Christine
You keep on building
That field of dreams
And don't stop
Until it's done
Remember they say
If you build it
It will come
But it won't
If you don't believe, hun
So choose
We're all in a position
To set the rules
Therefore it's up to us
Whether we win or lose
Just try your best
Not to get confused
Maybe you will

Maybe you won't
Share my views
It's your move
But if I was you
And looking for a way through
I know exactly what I would do
Never surrender
There's no excuse
Might as well face the truth
You're either in it to win it
Or you're in it to lose
Now some say
Just go with the flow
But going with the flow
Could mean ending up
Somewhere you didn't want to go
So let's learn to steer the boat
To the island of our dreams
Or end up washed up
Somewhere else downstream
Far away
From where we could have been
Get my drift
Seen
Let lost hope be redeemed
And let's be extra keen

To set deadlines
And meet them
Whether they arrive on time
Or not
Let's be there to greet them
With a dedication
That can't be beaten
Whatever the weather
Because it's now or never
The goal is open now
But it won't be forever
Therefore
We must endeavour
Or remain a part
Of the minor league
Never to proceed
Never to lead
Or reach our full potential
On the scoreboard
It's a tug of war
But we can't afford
Not to score
Because to miss this
Is to miss life's final four
So with only one chance
To make it

That rarely comes twice
We better take it
Or be losers
In this game
We call life.

THE NEXT LEVEL

You go day by day
Month by month
Year by year
Waiting and hoping
For your life to change
Meanwhile
The days go by
The months go by
And the years go by
Until we realise
Our life cannot change
While we stay the same
Becoming who you want to be
Requires moving on
From who you've been
You will only reach your next level
By letting go of where you are
You will only go as far
As you allow your imagination
To take you
Whenever we think
We've considered
And gone over
Everything it will take

To achieve our goals
Dreams
Ambitions
And desires
We must go over our list again
And add patience
The one missing ingredient
To a recipe for success
Is often just simply
Patience
We must stop looking at success
As a distant stranger
Instead
A nearby friend
Who is patiently
Awaiting our arrival
Follow your heart
And your instinct
They know you
Better than you think
I realised
I didn't like the world
As it was presented to me
So I'm taking the parts I do like
Adding some of my own making
And creating a whole new one

Seeing not what is
But what could be
And creating it
Too often
We die from the opinions
Of people
Whom we'll never meet
Often being strong
Is not in how long
We can hold on to things
But in how easily
We can let them go
Many of us
Spend our lives
Searching for happiness
In everything
But an altered state of mind
The only place
Where it is truly found
Some find happiness
Many make their own
Don't give up
Keep going
Often the ones
Who leave
While laughing at you

Come back later
Asking for your advice
I wish you the strength
To pick up
All of your broken pieces
And the patience
To put yourself back together again
I used to wish people the best
Now I wish them
Peace of mind
There's nothing better to have
Than that
There's a time to move swiftly
And a time to stand still
Knowing which to do
And when
Is everything
You are born exceptionally unique
And unlike anyone else
There will never ever
Be another human being
Who is wired exactly like you
We are all amazingly very different
There has never before in history
Been anyone just like you
And there will be

None to come after
So don't try to blend in
Stand out
You are a one of one
Always be yourself
And have faith in you
Know your worth
And the value of your abilities
Know who you are
And who you're not
It's time to push yourself
To the next level.

THE PROCESS OF TUNING IN

This is all
In the process
Of tuning in
Nothing shall be read
Or verbally expressed tonight
Only within
The deepest recesses
Of my mind
Will one find
What I am thinking
If one has true interest
He can begin
Linking
The rhymes
Which will unravel signs
But only for the distance
Of time
He travels
But only for the distance
Of time he travels
Can he begin linking
The rhymes
Which will unravel signs
If one has true interest

He will find
The deepest recesses
Of my mind
Tonight
Only within
Nothing shall be read
Or verbally expressed
This is all
In the process
Of tuning in.

THE TIMEPIECE

The clock ticks
Tick tock tick
Time is running out
Shit
Today is the beginning
Of the rest of my life
It is
So
What should I do with it
Furthermore
What should you do with it
With yours
Knowing that every day
Is another step towards
Death
Or as some call it
That transmission
All the loved ones
And things
You accumulated here
Would you miss them
Why are you here
What's your mission
Better make a decision

Tick tock tick
The clock ticks
Listen
Maybe you're waiting
Somewhere
In between the ticking
For someone
Or something
To tell you
Your life's purpose
Let's hope it's worth it
And not worthless
Wasted time
Waiting for a sign
When instead
You could decide
To find it within yourself
Sit on the shelf
But why
When you could decide
To find it within yourself
And rise into thy place
There really is no time
To waste
Because the clock ticks
Tick tock tick

Time is running out
Shit.

THE UNAWARE

As all types of strange phenomena
Surround the atmosphere
More wool is pulled over the eyes
Of the unaware
I wonder
Do any care
These days and nights
Are so cold here
I struggle
To walk with no fear
As the wicked eyes stare
I feel it in the air
The end is near
So I prepare
As unbelievers
Make a mockery
Of the revelations I see
They make a mockery
Of what could indeed be
Their own destiny
Staying ignorant
To the possibility
Of these things
Ever coming to be

Only the chosen
Understand the prophecies
As global catastrophes
Elevate towards
Their highest degrees
Spreading like disease
And multiplying like fleas
Some say times
Can't get worse than these
But we're living in the wicked city
The dark city
Wide, wide world with no pity
It's far from pretty
It's the final times
These could be my final lines
My final chance
To give sight back to the blind
And awaken the sleeping mind
There's still a long way to climb
I'm flirtatious with the rhyme
Because I see the signs
Some things are not right
Everything is not as it appears
The truth has been hidden
And has been so for years
By those

Who seek no less
Than absolute rule
What will become of the people
If they allow themselves
To be fooled
The unaware.

THIS IS NOT THE END

The plantations
That were green and rich
With vegetation
Have dried up
And been left fallow
The clean clear rivers
That once ran deep
Have now become polluted
And shallow
The birds
No longer perch
And sing here
For this barren land
Would only echo
Their loneliness
The air has become toxic
And unclean
So the trees
Are unable to breathe
Too weak in their boniness
The high rocky mountains
That once harboured life
Only serve now
As tombs to harbour decease

While the seemingly
Tormented
And abandoned
Desolate land beneath them
Seems to beckon
For release
The vultures
Gather here no more
For they too would die
And wither away
In this deserted place
Of calm unrest
Nothing can live here
So nothing stays here
Nothing can graze here
So nothing ever comes here
For fear of death
For as the season changes
The cold harsh windiness
Blows its dead
Into scattered bones
And then
Into nothingness
Then comes the sun again
That once made high stench
Of rotting flesh

Now boldly returning
To claim that
Which is left
New life will come here
To this land
Again and again
And die here
Naive
To the nature of it's trend
Only few
Will live long enough
To move on
And to see
That this
Is not the end.

TO THE FIRE

Wake up, Supernova
Rise and grind
If you want to shine
Then you've got to put in the time
If you haven't got to go to work
Then why get up at three
Because I love progress
More than I like sleep
Oh that's just way too early
I couldn't do that myself
Well then you just might
Spend the rest of your life
Working for someone else
I'm chasing my dreams
While I'm awake
I'll only miss
The opportunities I didn't take
I'll only lose
If my eyes aren't on the prize
Sacrifice is to choose paying a price
If only five percent are willing to give
Then only five percent will get
The other ninety-five
Will just have to accept whatever's left

Whatever's left is the result
Of anything other than my best
Do better to get better
Expect nothing less
Today
I seize the beast by the horns
My painted face to the storm
Naked as the day I was born
Deep in the thorns
Redeeming all the pieces of me
That were torn
This is the healing
Feeling like I'm reformed
I sit
Motionless
Beside you
And at times
As if outside of myself
Looking down
I watch you
Sleeping
Unknowing
Incoherent
Unconscious
I wonder
About everything it might take

To fully restore you back to life
Even greater than before
I see you now
And know that
All the treasure in the world
Can't compare
To that which is truly alive
You
You deserve more
We fantasised
About winning the lottery
And with the money
All the things we'd do
It's funny I didn't realise
I'd already landed the jackpot
The very day that I won you
There isn't another soul
That I can blame
I threw our winning ticket
To the fire
Watched it go up in flames
You've probably
Burned everything I have
Like I burned everything we had
I'm so ashamed
You fell in love with who I was

Then I pretended
To be someone else
You didn't fall for it
Thank god
I was only fooling myself
A false alarm only I can hear
Inside of a me
Only you can see
A gold spoon
In an empty room
A precious flower
Blossomed too soon
I pray you never know
What that feels like
A stifled scream
In the dead of night
To the fire now
Burn bright
Don't close your eyes
You'll miss the lights
Did a few things
That I shouldn't have done
But done a lot more
That I'm glad I did
What you're aiming for is hard to hit
If you don't know what the target is

And the hardest bit
Is learning
That you were easy work
Yet I so easily
And naively
Made it hard
For us to work
For what it's worth
With
Or without you
It hurts
I feel so deeply entangled
Within my thoughts right now
I can barely piece together words
Tell me
How to craft a worthy
Patchwork remedy
For a broken melody
I'll cast my lot here
And plant a soapbox at your feet
Everyday
Until it sparks a memory
Finally
Speaking without interruption
And now without any idea
Of what more I can say

If I ever told people
I've been coming here to visit you
They'd probably try to put me away
Throw me in some kind of
Mental institute
Some asylum somewhere
For people supposedly
Outside of their minds
Lock us both up
And melt down the key
All just because
They'd never ever find
Among all their precious boxes
One to fit us in
You know
They say
It's not at all about what you know
But what we know
Is it's not who you know
It's who you know who actually gives a shit
Nobody in the world
Cares about your
Grand schemes
And dreams
But you
Yourself

And you
That's it
That's at least until
You can make
Those dreams come true
So make it happen
Take action
Because there's satisfaction
In even a fraction that you do
Show and prove
Paint your city
Make it pretty
And capture the views
Spectacular views
See everything to gain
With absolutely nothing to lose
But the blues
And if you actually do
You'll see this
To be factually true
Alteration in your navigation
Makes your map improve
If you don't like
Where your life is at
Then that's for you
The right solution

To your life's improvement
Lies in wise decisions
And their execution
Let's keep it moving
Little by little makes a lot
It's all about progression
Give it everything you've got
Who laughs doesn't matter
And who matters doesn't laugh
Your task
Is to double up
On what you're doing
Versus how much you care
All you do is keep going
They wont be laughing
When you're there
Architect of your own destiny
Your own future by design
Naysayers keep checking in
Tell them you haven't got the time
And if people
Expect to offer you less
Than you're giving
Then they should expect
That you decline
That's fine

Know your worth
And that the best things
Come to those who work
Earn and live
Live and earn
But nothing comes close
To the gifts you can give
From the things you've learned
Your bridges they can burn
And your tides can turn
But never giving up
Is your only concern
Those who give up on you
Can't expect to get down with you
When you get up
And in this
You can trust for sure
Support is everything
But loyalty
And respect is more
Never forget
What you got in for
For keeps
So dig yourself deep
And explore
Until you find the missing piece

Remember
All things are possible
And nothing is beyond reach
You've heard this all before
I've been saying it in your sleep
And I know you've been listening
Because above the noise
And the toil
I can still hear your heart beat
And inside
I can still feel it
Like it's a part of me
Coming alive
Breathing renewed life
And bleeding new light
Into my existence
Who am I
But a guy
Standing by
Just to witness its brilliance
You could ask me why
But to see you shine
Has been my only mission
And in this instance
I just need you to hide your disguise
Put all your fears and pride aside

And listen
Let your will be strong
Make your will
Stronger than your won't
You won't go wrong
You will succeed where others don't
Believe in yourself
And your abilities
And what you can achieve
And if you can't see your greatness
Or your potential
Believe in someone who sees
Sees it in you
Someone who wont be leaving
Until you see it too
And you profess that it's true
That you're the perfect catalyst
To manifest every gift
You've been blessed with
You
Yes
You've already been
At your deepest darkest depths
That's nothing new
Embark towards
Your highest

Brightest heights yet
You already know what to do
Let your mind be free
Explore each
And every possibility
There's so much more to see
Be who you're supposed to be
You can be down to earth
Or be up to space
Know that your worth
Is much more
Than the world dictates
Feet firmly on the ground
On route to Mars
Your time is now
Be who you are
At one among the stars
A new point of view
You see what you feel
New practices
New politics
New playing field
Stretch yourself
Play for real
Invest in yourself
Make a deal

But of course
I'm a modern day renaissance man
Born in London in the late seventies
What do I know
I know
That if you put your mind to anything
Over time it grows
And so
I'm seeing live with my own eyes
Mere dreams
Turning into real life
I'm encountering souls
Overcoming their own status quos
I'm witnessing
The attainment of goals
I'm seeing doors open wide
That used to stay closed
I'm hearing Yes expressed
Where I used to hear No's
Get up
I've heard too much
And I've seen too much
And I know too much
To just let you go
I can't
And I won't

I'm sorry
But I love you
A gold spoon
In an empty room
A precious flower
Blossomed too soon
I pray you never know
What that feels like
A stifled scream
In the dead of night
To the fire now
Burn bright
Don't close your eyes
You'll miss the lights
Molotov cocktails
In flight
Look like baby fireflies
At this height
What on earth
Could ever be wrong
When after all is said and done
And all have sang and gone
All that will be left
Is this love song to ponder on
All of this high frequency rhetoric
All this poetry

Yes it's poetic
But it's more phonetic energy
Helping me
Set free
All of what I'll never need
Permanently
Forgetting more
Of what I've learned to be
While other mad men
Would walk towards
The edge of eternity
Just to capture
Only a glimpse of you
In the tail end
Of a moon beam
I wake to discover you
Here with me
And absolutely
No part of a dream
You're the heart of me
And the most beautiful thing
In this universe
I've ever seen
You are awesomeness
Incredibly
And wonderfully made

And not by mistake
You are greatness
Personified on the planet
Why are you waiting to be great
Find a way
Or one way make
From there keep straight
And for greatness sake
Try not to arrive late
By your own thoughts
And by your own actions
You'll determine your fate
Throughout all of existence
That which doesn't create
Disintegrates
We've been given rise
Over every tall tree
And over every high place
So it makes no sense to me
Who would ever decide
To only grow halfway
That's only my take though
What do you say
Like who remembers
The embers anyway
What of the smouldering remains

After the glowing beauty
Of the flames
It all melts down
Burns out
Change is the only thing
That stays the same
Ashes to ashes
To the death
Of everything before
Toast to the old ways
Yesterday
A far away spark in the dark
Today a blaze
Wake up, Supernova
Welcome the new day.

TO WHOM IT MAY CONCERN

You knew you were wrong
But still you persisted
Your conscience pricked you
But still you resisted
On and on
You pursued that
Which you knew
Would bring harm
Inside your heart raced
But outside you played calm
For if they saw
For a second
The truth
That was hidden in you
Counteracted
Would be all
That you were trying to do
You sought so many ways
To justify your actions
But to no avail
And to no satisfaction
I heard a man say once
That such people will burn
This is of course

To whom it may concern

Since you willed
Such things to happen
Without raising a hand
Towards prevention
It is fair then to say
The outcome of such things
Has been your intention
And that if there should be
A day and a place
Where all good people
Are mentioned
You shall not be among them
Or be brought
To their attention
It's intense
In the way
That you have neglected
Your inner voices
Urging you
To change your focus
And make different choices
As far as you're concerned
Your agenda is set
And you've made up your mind

Many will forgive
But none will forget
And indeed there will come a time
The days of your name
Shall be blown away
Like the feathers of a fern
This is of course
To whom it may concern

Your decisions
Have caused
Much suffering
And pain
You even hurt yourself
As well as those around you
Under the strain
You cared not
What knowledgeable people said
Would be for the best
You carried on
Inconsiderate
And indifferent nevertheless
It's important to see the karma here
In order to make a change
Or grow
You will only reap

What you have sown here
And this the farmer does know
Realise
That all the good you do
Will be recorded
Against your name
And that likewise
All the bad you do
Will be recorded just the same
For it is through the consequences
Of his actions
That each soul shall learn
And of course
This is
To whom it may concern.

TOMORROW

You hear that?
That's the sound
Of daylight creeping in
A new day is coming
A better day is on its way
Tomorrow is a better day
Believe that
I thought this day
Would never come
Thought we'd never see the sun
Thinking of all those
Wrong turns I made
That turned out
To be right turns
And I'm left
Turning it over
Inside my mind
It's just a familiar place
I like to visit sometimes
Because it's crazy
When you really think about it
I don't know
What I would've done without it
The discipline

To know the difference
The discernment
To have taken
A different position
Seeing it for what it really is
And what it really isn't
Clear vision
Not blinded
By your own insistence
And limited thinking
Resistance
All the obstacles you face
That are often put in place
To completely
Slow down your pace
When you're too busy
Speeding ahead
All systems go
Thinking it's a race
When often
Exactly what you need
Is to slow down
Stop and listen
In order to know
Exactly what to do
And where to go

And what to say
Abort mission
Go this way
Go that
But that was yesterday
Today
All I can say
Is only if we knew then
What we know now
If only today knew us
Like tomorrow knows us
Just one more day
Just one more day
I see a bright morning ahead
Yes
That's what I said
Clear skies all the way
Just one more day
Brighter days are on the way
I feel so good right now
So good
It's like an awesome awakening
My head realised
The rehearsal
Is the actual thing
And my heart

Just wants to sing
I feel like a part of everything
The start
The middle
And the ending
A morning chorus to the King
For all that tomorrow brings.

TOUCH THE SUN

We slave away
For paydays
Just so we can pay
For rainy days
With the little money we've saved
Praying for a pay raise
Meanwhile
The tax man
Is preying
On what we've made
While we spend
More than we're paid
Buy more than we sell
Give more than we take
And for some
It's a living hell
And we just might break
From not coping too well
But we smoke
And drink well
And don't know
If you can tell
But we're trying
To numb the pain

Hoping things will get better
We used to run to the door
For Valentine's
And love letters
Now we run and hide
From bills
And debt collectors
We used to go out
But now we're trapped in
Behind a pile of red letters
From buying
As many things
As our bad credit would let us
And who would help us
Sooner than forget us
Like dust to dust
Good friends
Just blow away
On our bad days
Like who can we trust
But why should we fuss
When we can breathe easy
And remind ourselves
That we can be eternal
That's priceless
Why should we cuss

When all that matters
Is remembering
That what's precious
About our existence
Is internal
That's what life is
Why should we be pissed
Gold and silver
Fades away
And all the riches
In the world
Couldn't buy this
A chance to touch the sun
And uncover the god
In everyone
And though the devil's work
Is never done
I see the potential
In everyone
To let go and grow
Towards all we aim to become
To reach out and glow
As we touch the sun.

TRUTH ABOUT MONEY

It is said
Money isn't everything
But people without it
Want enough money
To be able
To form their own judgement
Many say
Money doesn't grow on trees
But I've learned
If you're smart enough
You can make money grow anywhere
It is said
Money doesn't buy happiness
At the very least
People want enough money
To be able to afford
To pay for the illusion that it does
Many swear
Money itself
Is the root of all evil
But in a world
Where money rules
No goodness can come
From being without.

WE WILL SURVIVE

Fell asleep
Woke up
As one among
81 serenity souls
Captured
In the inevitable mystique
Of sound
Wearing scars on our backs
From bearing
So many blessings
Took counsel from healers
Then spoke
As if we'd walked
The entire universe
In a stare
A blink
A whisper
Or passing phase
Spent time
Handing out lifelines
In sentences
Creating progressive lifetimes
In days
Whilst mastering

How to shape
Shift
In and out of words
Words
That made mankind
Want to make more of his mind
Words
That made many
Want to make more money
Words
That made many
Motivated
To move more mountains
Words
That made men more weary
Words
That made women
Want for more
Because we knew
It was the only way
We would survive
The only way
We would survive
Like we survived slavery
Survived slave ships
Survived chains

Survived whips
Survived lynching
Survived burning
Survived punching
Survived kicks
Survived rape
Survived castration
Survived fields
Where our blood ran
As cotton was picked
Had to survive
Still have to survive
Survive the struggle
Of the divide
Into poor and rich
Survive the reverse
Of god to dog
And goddess to bitch
Survive aids
Survive guns
Survive alcohol
Survive drugs
Survive prison
And wrongful arrest
Survive hate
Survive anguish

Survive pain
Coming together
Living forever
Surviving death
Because we have to survive
We must survive
We've got to survive
We will
Survive.

WONDER OF THE SOUL

I often wonder
If the soul
Is aware of itself
Beyond this earthly shell
We call the human body
I wonder
After we die
Does our soul
Remember our names
Who we were
Where we've been
And what we've seen
And experienced in life
Or whether it just
Leaves any memory of us
Behind completely
I wonder
If it is aware of us anymore
Or just of itself
And where it is bound.

WRITTEN WARNING

If you
Should be so fated
To fall in love
With a writer
Be sure it is love
And love them truly
It is a burden to bear
To love
Such an individual as this
But love them
Wholeheartedly
Love them fully
Love them
Unashamedly
And deeply
Withdraw and flee
From their presence
Immediately
If it is not so
Or if it is not in you
To love them
Freely
And completely
For the mighty sword

They are fated to wield
Gives birth
To both life and death
Thus
Do not deceive them
Do not lie
Do not love them falsely
Conditionally
Or uncertainly
For if they decide
You have intentionally
Mislead
Mistreated
Or wronged them
They will immortalise you
In all the places
Where words are found
Or in one place
Where you'll burn
Forever
Where you will live long
But painfully
And die slowly
And miserably
You will be eternally
Reincarnated

In a poem
On a wall
On a page
In a book
In a film
In a song
On a stage
Out of a mouth
Into an ear
You will scream
Inside yourself
Suffering silently
At the sight
Of your own resemblance
You'll be rewritten
And replayed
Reborn
Then reborn again
Only to live
Forevermore
Spending rereads
And reruns
Of those
Miserable lifetimes
Wishing
You could just die.

ABOUT THE AUTHOR

Phoenix James is an award winning Writer, Poet, Author and Spoken Word Recording Artist. He began performing his poetic words live on stages across the UK in 1998. His debut spoken word poetry album, *The A.R.T.I.S.T,* was released in 2000. His first limited edition printed collection of poetry, *To Whom It May Concern,* was published in 2003. He has toured and performed his poetry internationally since 2004. He has appeared in films, on television and radio shows, and collaborated with other artists, singer-songwriters, actors, musicians, filmmakers and producers. In 2013, he wrote, directed and produced the feature length mock documentary film, *Love Freely but Pay for Sex.* Phoenix James has written, recorded and released several spoken word poetry albums including, *Phenzwaan Now & Forever* (2009), *A Patchwork Remedy for A Broken Melody* (2020), *FREE* (2021), *Haven for the Tormented* (2021), *With All That Said* (2022), and *Remixes* Volumes: 1 & 2 (2022).

If you enjoyed reading this book, please leave a review online. The author reads every review and they help new readers discover his work.

PHOENIX JAMES

Photo by Phoenix James

Phoenix James lives in London, England.

Connect with Phoenix James on his online social media platforms via www.linktr.ee/ Phoenix_James and say you've read this book. To contact or learn more about Phoenix James and his creative journey or to receive updates via his Newsletter Mailing List, visit his official website at www.PhoenixJamesOfficial.com

Phoenix James Official

WE ALL SHOULD BE AMAZED

A Collection of Poetry and Spoken Word

PJ

PHOENIX JAMES

WE ALL SHOULD BE AMAZED

For any questions about usage, please email contact@PhoenixJamesOfficial.com

First Edition: 2025

ISBN: 978-1-0685383-3-9 (Paperback)
ISBN: 978-1-0685383-4-6 (Ebook)

Cover Artwork & Design by Phoenix James.
Book Design & Formatting by Phoenix James.

Visit the author's website at www.PhoenixJamesOfficial.com or email him at phoenix@PhoenixJamesOfficial.com

DEDICATION

For you, the seeker of light
Who still looks up and wonders
Who finds stories in the stars
And miracles
In the quiet corners of the day

For you, who refuses to stop feeling
Who has carried tears like rivers
And found in their salt
The shimmer of truth
The quiet of healing
The proof of being alive

For every heart astonished
By beauty in broken places
By the miracle of connection
By the magic that lingers
In every breath
These words are yours

And to a radiant young boy
May they be a mirror
A lantern
A gentle hand on your shoulder
May they remind you, always
That the world is more than it seems
That wonder waits everywhere
And that you
Are part of its astonishment.

CONTENTS

AMAZING AT THE GATE

We struggle
We strive
We thrive
We stay alive
We survive
We make it
To the next day
To say we did okay
Hey, that wasn't so bad
Let's go another day
Let's continue along the way
The nights are dark
And the days are hot
Nothing was ever comfortable
I kid you not
But giving up
Is the worst thing
We could do right now
We've come so far
And we should be proud
We made it out
From where we were
Nothing is perfect
No dream deferred

We're on the move
And we're moving loud
But moving in silence
That just means the crowd
They hear
They see
They witness
They comment
And they critique
We keep it moving
Whoever thought this could be
We should be amazed
Look how far we came
Look how far we've come
We all should be amazed
For what we've done
We didn't cave
Amazing at the gate
And we didn't succumb
Beautiful are we
Like stars in the sky
And there we shine
Not a soul on earth
Could say that we didn't try
Not a soul anywhere
Could say that we didn't fly.

AT END OF PLAY

She flows across my mind
Drowning my heated thoughts
Like cool water
On a hot sunshine day
Washing over my body
And my soul
She is the purple rain
The purple haze
The indigo
And in I go
High and bright
Like the great sky light
Shining at its height
Glistening across her pool
A shimmering fine delight
Water cool blue
Hot brown skin
I'm just a fool
Caught up in her whirlwind
She comes
She goes
To where only heaven knows
All I ever know

Is I'm the one she chose
To bring sun to shadows
On nights like those
Which brings some to me
On days like these
I take what I need
Their warmth
Their heat
And then set them free
Because nothing stays
Most of all
Not she
Not her
Not them
Not me
We
Each fade away
At end of play
At the end of the day
She said
Her syrup kisses were forever
I begged her to differ
As that would be a pleasure
But they will only exist
For as long as we remember
The reasons we endeavour

And like palm trees in a hurricane
We held on
And held on
And became strong again
Through strong winds
Through heavy rains
Until calmer days maintained
And seasons changed
To bright skies blue
And a clear water view
With sunlight shining through
Palm trees and greenery
Now looking like new
That's the way it seems to me
Now looking at you
Within a different pursuit
A new lens to see through
New and improved
And focused
From deep within
Sweet melanin coated skin
Finally seeing everything
She didn't notice a thing
Like a passer-by
Inside a dream
We were a split team

Caught in a slipstream
We fought in a big ravine
We thought we'd stay afloat in
Only to be swallowed in the ocean
When the cruel tide rolled in
Although we tried
We couldn't swim
We all die
So many times like this
Without realising
Feelings slip in and slip out
Like catching a fistful of water
Caresses turn to clenched fists
Smiles turn to gritted teeth
War starts when the truth ends
Men yearn for a distant peace
Far away from the activism
It's here
And I'm at ease
Washes over me like a baptism
Setting a captive free.

BEYOND LUST

For once, I don't want to
Strip you naked
For once, your curves
Are not the main focus
For once, I'm focused more
On your energy
Than your nakedness
And your mind
More than your orgasms
For once, I just want
To be still
And hold you
For once, I just want
To look at you
Through eyes
That are not lustful
Into eyes
That are beautiful
Beyond sex
I just want
To stay in this moment
That we've created
Still fully clothed
And just held

And where
There's no need
For anything
Other than stillness
There's no anxiousness
No rush of lust
No raging hormones
Just the stillness
Of the moment
In an embrace
In a conversation
Where the idea
Of physical lovemaking
Is far away from our minds
And because
They've already
Been whisked away
In a sublime distraction
Of mental interaction
On a whole other level
Way above that
And it's magical
That for once with you
I'm stimulated by
A side of you
That is not wanton

And wet
And sticky
And moaning
But a side of you
That for once
Is open
In a far more
Simulating way.

BLOCKBUSTER VIDEO

I don't really worry about it too much
When there's something I want to watch
I just rent it online there and then
It's like the old days
Of the Blockbuster Video store
When you just used to go
And choose a movie
Rent the VHS tape
Take it home
Watch it, and take it back
Wow, imagine that
You would have never, ever imagined
There was something in the future
Where you'd be able
To go onto a computer
Look at a screen
And download
Or pay for online
A movie
Where you wouldn't even
Have to physically touch
A VHS tape
Or go outside to a store

Just from your own home
It's all done online
No handling cash
No returning or collecting a tape
From the video shop
Who would ever
Have thought then
That it would be as it is now
No more Blockbuster Video.

BRAZEN MERMAIDS

I came across you again
Some other day
Out fishing again
At the hypergamy market
Where we all starfish
For chips, cheese, and a wet chain
You captured my attention
And articulated my mind frame
Into tangled seaweed
So many of my personal thoughts
Thrown out to see
If I've grown over the years
Or if they've grown over me
Those strangling weeds
Either way, none groan over me
While swimming the wild waters
Wherein one should be cautious
I'm guessing you're passing through
Just like all the brazen mermaids do
Hoping to catch one on the way down
Another nice strong young wet one
Falling for yet another slippery tongue
With less experience of the sea

To slip deep into your wide net
When you should really let it be
But you'll keep him hooked there
Until you're either bored or satisfied
And ready to set him free.

BUYING SIGNS

Although
I don't buy into star signs
And all of that fully
When you get the newspaper
And it says
This is your horoscope today
I don't fully buy into all of that
But on the zodiac side
And like certain traits
Matching a person
I can even say for myself
Certain Virgo traits
That I read about
The main thread
The ones I see all the time
Right across the board
About Virgos
I can definitely say
That I can relate to them
And I can see myself
In those descriptions of a Virgo
Very much so
And although I don't buy into it all fully

I do see that
And also, I think
In terms of the earth
And how there's
Different seasons for things
And how the planet works
And how the moon affects the ocean
And we're made up
Of seventy percent water
And the earth is as well
I feel we're definitely affected
By what's going on, on the planet
So that's the side where I buy into it
Where there is truth in it, to me
Because of the way
We're affected by the earth
And our behaviour is affected
And how the full moon
Affects our moods and behaviours
So there are elements that I do accept
There are things outside of us
That are happening
That when they talk about the zodiac
And the moon
And the stars
And everything

Us being affected by that
Undeniably
I do buy into a lot of that
Because of the facts of it.

CERTAIN THINGS

Although I say
All things should be tried
In this big, wide world
Of wonderful experiences
In this short life
I also feel, for myself personally
I have an addictive personality
So therefore
Certain things I shouldn't try
Because I will enjoy them too much
And they may take me away
From what I should be doing
Actually doing
Not just for enjoyment
That's one of my thoughts
But aside from that
I think everything should be tried
And enjoyed
As much as possible
I just might start roller skating
Or something else addicting
And not finishing my books.

DATES & ADVERTISING SPACE

When I joined the dating apps
I joined with the intention
Of wanting to meet someone new
I was coming out of a relationship
And spent six months by myself
Kind of finding myself again
And then decided
It was time to meet someone
You kind of miss that intimacy
And that closeness
And that conversation
And those nice, warm
Cozy nights in with someone
You kind of miss all that stuff
So I decided
That I was then ready
To get out there
And start dating again
That's how it started
With joining the dating apps
Following on from that
You put on what you do on there
Your work

Your interests
Then interest came from that
And then I just decided
It was somewhere
That I could also share what I do more
And promote my work
Especially if it's a space
That you're paying for
Then it's advertising space
It has absolutely become that as well
For me, for sure
Being there
Has often led to new readers
And new fans of my work
Without a doubt
But it's definitely not the reason I joined
It's just become part of being there
And I accept it, and embrace it
I don't shy away from it at all
I definitely make use of the space
In that regard
As well as dating
I can't knock it
For additional eyeballs
Or attention
On what I do professionally.

FEAR OF ARTIFICIAL INTELLIGENCE

It's something that
Was a fear to me initially
But I think since
I've got to understand more about it
And as more time has gone on
I feel that I see it
As more of a friend now
Rather than something to fear
More of a tool
When I think about
All the good it can do
As opposed to all the negative
I feel that there's so much
That AI will allow us to do
That benefits us
As opposed to being a threat
Or something to fear
Like the robots are going to kill us
That whole thing
I just feel it's an advancement
In technology
That we can use
To better our communication

Preservation of ourselves
And our thoughts and our ideas
Our families and our history
And our ancestry
And all of that
I just feel it's a tool for speed
Documentation in general
I just feel
There are so many benefits to it
That often don't get looked at
Because of this fear of
Oh, the robots are going to kill us
And technology
Is taking over our jobs
And our lives
I feel there are way more benefits
That are not really
Being looked at now
Because it's early
But it's the same thing as before
With everything else
The telephone
The car
The airplane
There was always someone
Opposing these new ideas

And still are, a lot of them
But there's so much more
That we're going to gain from it
I think as always, like everything else
It can be used for good or evil
I think people will agree
There's so many benefits
To smart technology
If we look at our smart phones
And what we're able to do
With these devices
And the speed it gives us
And time saving
And being in touch with relatives
Who are far away
And that is great
Just that alone is a benefit
That you couldn't have had
Prior to that ability
Through technology
So I think AI
Is going to bring lot of good
And I'm embracing that more
Than I was initially
So I'm looking forward to
Embracing change

Because it's inevitable for one
And I'm alive
And as long as I don't allow
The fear part of it
To take over me
I can really move with the times
And benefit
From what has to offer
Right now I feel good about AI
Really good in fact
I think with everything
That comes into the human sphere
I think that humans
Are good and bad
And I think that AI
Being this new thing
Will bring the good and bad
Out of people
I think it will be used for good
And it will be used for bad
And that's the humans
That's not AI
It's change
And change is always scary.

FOR ALL TIME

I love the iconic figures
I watched as a kid
Like Audrey Hepburn
And Marilyn Monroe
And so on
We'll all be forgotten
Eventually
In the sands of time
Even the most famous
And influential of us
Or maybe not
Maybe since their era
And others like them
We've found a way
To preserve ourselves
For all time
Maybe
Maybe not
Perhaps the earth
Will take it all back one day
To dust
Everything
But since you're reading this
I guess they survived.

GATEWAY TO THE NEXT

I've always said that
Every time I've said in my mind
At least even if
I've not said it outwardly
That this is it
This is the thing
It's what I'm meant to do for life
I found the thing
That I'm meant to be doing
It's always evolved
And changed
Even the way I was doing a thing
Changed and evolved
Into something else
And I realised
That one special thing
That everything I did
Was the gateway to the next thing
And enough times that's happened
To make me see
That it's always only the gateway
To the next thing
So even what I'm doing now

I see as the gateway to the next thing
Although writing and poetry
Has always been the thread
Through all of that
I never saw film
I never saw video
I never saw music
I never saw theatre
I never saw any of it
But one has always been
The gateway to the next
I guess writing will always be there
It's fluid
I mean, essentially the DNA is writing
And expression of that
And the skill, yeah
But where that will go
Is going to be somewhere else
It will evolve into another place
That's in the future
I don't know what it is yet
I didn't know what the others were
Time shows me
When it's time
To go through the next gate
Pretty cool.

HIP HOP AT THE TOP

I think my most influential genre
Of music
Would have to be...
It's a tough one
But I would say it's hip hop music
And I'll tell you why
Because of the words
Because of the lyrics
And because of the passion
And the expression
But I could quite easily
Say that about soul music as well
I guess I put hip hop above that
Because there's more words
Said in a rap song
As opposed to like a soul song
The passion is there
But the amount
Of words expressed
Is less
Obviously, you're going to feel
More things by each line
I am a person

That strongly appreciates words
And meanings
And language
And expression
So I think I say hip hop music
For the storytelling
The creative rhymes
And the messages
In the hip hop music
I've learned a lot from
And have been inspired by
And I've been educated by
And entertained
So definitely hip hop
Because of the amount of content
In there words wise
To listen and learn and understand
And I think for that reason
But in saying that
I get that from probably
Every other music that has lyrics in it
But hip hop probably would be the top
And for those reasons
And then closely followed
By soul music
And the Blues

Any music
That has that kind of passion
And soul in it
I guess because hip hop music
Is so conversational
It's speaking
It's speaking with rhyme
I get it more from that
Than I would
By someone singing the words
But the feeling is there still
I just would put hip hop music
Just above
For the conversational aspect
Not to say it's absent
From the other genres
But when someone's rapping
It's words being fired at you
It's very engaging in that sense
And this has also been
Where my passion
For poetry came from
And poetry
Is an evolution
Of my early days of rapping
Which came

From listening to hip hop music
So there's that too
I just began performing my lyrics
Without music in the end
And that became
More termed as poetry
Being on stage
And just saying words that rhymed
So that's quite interesting as well
And how much of an influence
It's actually been.

IN NEED OF A GOOD BATH

Do you know
What I haven't had for a long time
Too long, in fact
I may need to make
Specific arrangements
So that I can have it again soon
But I haven't had a bath
For a long time
Like in a bathtub
Soaking in the bath
With candles
And foam and bubbles
And music
And a cool drink
Just relaxing
Immersed
Laying back in a bathtub
I haven't done that for a long time
Because I don't have a bathtub
I have a shower
And the last time
I was in a bathtub
Was in Egypt
In the hotel
And just really appreciating

The luxury of that moment
Because I have a shower back home
So that was the last time
That was quite some time ago
I really do miss being in the bathtub
And just steaming my body
In that moment
That hot water full of bubbles
And just enjoying it
Just relaxing back
Haven't done that for so long
I need to just book something like that
Or go somewhere that has a tub
And just enjoy that
It's a luxury
When you don't actually have one
I think we take it for granted
When we have things
And then not having them
You just, wow, yeah
I need to experience that
I need to just...
I used to get
Such a therapeutic experience
From that.

IN THE GOING DOWN

Life is so brief
That we only realise it
At the end
And it's sad
It's sad that
We don't see
The things
That really matter
Until it's towards
The end of that life.

IN THE SURRENDER

Nothing truly waits for us
Only the empty spaces
We resist embracing
We wander endlessly
Through time
Chasing arrival
Unaware
That we've always been
Exactly
Where we need to be
What do you feel
Pulling at you
In the quiet
Between everything else
Have you ever
Touched a moment
So still
It felt like it knew your name
What part of you
Longs to be seen
Even in silence
Is there a space inside you
That's been waiting
For you to come home

When was the last time
You surrendered
To the moment
Fully
Completely
If time
Paused right now
What
Would it catch you feeling
Have you ever
Mistaken longing
For movement
When stillness
Was where
The answer lived.

JUST LIKE YOU

In response
It will be worth considering
That the old fashioned chaps
And chics
Who went clubbing
And partying
In order to socialise
Are now today's weirdos
And wimps
Who are also on dating apps
Just like you now are
Back then
They didn't have a choice
But to be out
Socially interacting
If they wanted to meet people
Any dating app now
Is in fact
The new widely used form
Of social interaction
Dating app users
Are just everyday people
Both good and bad

That you'd meet anywhere
Out socially in person
Who might just happen
To also be on a dating app
Like you.

LEGACY LANGUAGE

They ask
Why is he so popular
As if it is hype
As if it is trend
As if twenty years of truth-telling
Heartbreak-healing
And line-breaking lyricism
Could be boxed into a hashtag
No
He is not popular
He's resonant
He is what happens
When pain turns into poetry
When silence
Becomes sound
When independence
Becomes empire
He didn't wait for a label
Didn't beg for a seat
He carved a path
From the pavement
With words
That made the broken breathe

Some artists entertain
He awakens
Some follow trends
He leads truths
He's not just a brand
He's a body of work
A mirror
A movement
You don't scroll past him
You stop
And feel
And that's why
He's known
Not because he wanted fame
But because he gave his name
To something greater
A legacy
A language
A reminder
That we're all still rising.

LIKE WATER

It's actually happening right now
It's happening right now
And it's what I was saying
Just before you handed over to me
That listening to you explain
About capoeira
As a form of martial art
And the history of it
I realised that I like your mind
And that's what's happening
Right this minute
The question you're asking
About what draws me in
What pulls me
Is happening right now
It's happening in real time
I'm being drawn to you more
By listening to you speak
And hearing your mind
And I'm interested
In what you were talking about
That really interests me
Because these are things
That I know a little about

But not a lot
Things that I'm interested in
You're talking about history
You're talking about language
You're talking about learning
Which is very important to me
About how around the colonial period
That enslaved Africans
Developed their capoeira
To not show their enslavers
That they were fight training
To defend themselves
That's amazing
I'm not sure I knew
That was the reason for it
This is interesting to me
And this knowledge
Is coming from your mind
And I'm listening to you
Looking at you
So what you just asked me
I'm in that moment right now
That's the first one
That comes to mind
Because it's happening right now
But if I was to go outside of this moment

To look for something like that
I guess learning is one of them
Because I love to learn
I love to expand my brain
Art is that
And creativity
Which I do a lot of
Writing, and the places it takes me
I'm constantly pulled by that
My own
And by that of others
For example, the African art piece
I asked you about
That you had displayed
That was interesting to me
It pulled me, it drew me in
I wanted to learn more about it
Where did it come from
So that's an example
But I'm really drawn in
And moved by art and creativity
And writing and song
And anything creative pulls me
And I draw from all of it
Music, film
And I put that all

Under the umbrella of art
That's what is in my DNA
That's what I breathe
Always
And to answer your other question
That's my support system
Because I'm in the world
And the world is that
And I draw from the world
Not in a sense of family
More in a sense of
It was in me already
And everything lit me up
That was around me
Everything fed it
And it was strong enough in me
That it didn't matter
Whether I had a supportive environment
I was going to gravitate to it anyway
And it's in my DNA
In the sense of it's how I compute
It's how I'm wired
So whatever's going on
Supportive environment or not
I'm still going to find a way
Like water.

LIQUEUR CONNOISSEUR

I only see drinking liqueurs
As making sense
When it comes to alcohol
I have a sweet tooth
Always have done
Not interested in wines
Lagers, beers
Gins and vodkas
I like sweet drinks, that is it
I don't see the point, otherwise
My favourite liqueur
Is probably going to be Disaronno
Baileys, Chambord, Midori, Archers
Malibu, even Southern Comfort
Because it's got that sweetness to it
And many more
But liqueurs for sure
I like them straight
I like them chilled, if possible
If not, room temperature
Never ice
I find that sacrilege
Abomination

I feel that putting ice in a drink
Especially a liqueur
Impairs the flavour
It waters it down
I think if it was intended
To have ice in it
It would be made like that
It would have been
Watered down to that degree
I believe if it's going to be cold
If that's the reason for the ice
It should be chilled beforehand
So it doesn't need ice
I will drink it warm
Before I put an ice cube in it
One hundred percent.

LOVING WORDS

My love of it came from
Just being a kid
And being so curious
And loving language
And loving the way
Words were delivered
In whatever it might be
A cartoon, a movie
Just television
Just loving that
Loving songs, music
And I had audio cassettes
I'd listen to
Just loving language
And loving words
Loving expression
I just always loved that
And books
Reading books
And the stories
Always loved that so much
And that's never left
That childhood appreciation
And love of that
Has always remained.

MRS. RIGHT AND I

Where I'm at right now
If there's a Mrs. Right
Out there for me
I'm happy to meet her
Because if she's right
She's right
And that'd be great
And I imagine
I'd be Mr. Right for her
I have no problem with that
I'd much rather have
All in any 'one night stands' with her
If that's at all possible
Who wouldn't
Who wouldn't want to have
The Mr. or Mrs. Right for themselves
And have all their
One night stand delights
With that one person
That's where I'm at with that
But am I chasing looking for her
Am I holding out for her
Not so much

No, I'm enjoying my life
And having a good time
With people
Who are on the same page as me
Who want to have a good time
And have fun as well
I am not actively pursuing marriage
Or any serious relationship at this point
I'm coming from
A serious relationship or two
In the past few years
But definitely not at this phase of my life
I'm kind of enjoying where I am
And putting myself in the places
Where I can be found
By her
Or by anyone else
Who's kind of feeling
On the same wavelength
And who connects with me
On the same level
Has the same chemistry as me
And wants to have a good time
That's kind of where I'm at right now
I'm open and in flow
And when it's right, it's right

And there's no demands
On anybody
To be anything for me
And hopefully, vice versa
And it works that way right now.

MY MAILBOX BIT ME

So I'm heading out one morning
I go to my mailbox
The same way I always do
My mailbox requires a key
So for a while now
Instead of using the key
For quickness
I would just put my hand
In the mouth of the mailbox
Just to check and see
If there is any mail there
Just because it was quicker
Than actually unlocking the box
So I put my fingers in the mouth
Into the tray to feel for mail
And on this particular day
When I went to pull my hand out
It decided to bite me
It was like, Nope
I'm keeping your hand
So my fingers were stuck in there
I pulled my hand out
Not as carefully as I should have

And then I looked
And saw my hand was bleeding
Blood by now was just pouring
The mouth of the letter box part
Is made of metal
And the sharp upper flap
Just caught the top
Of my middle finger
As I pulled my hand out
It said, not today
You've been doing this for too long
I'm going to teach you a lesson
You have a key, use it
And that's what went down
Just an accident
Carelessness on my part
As I was rushing out that day
And my mailbox
Was obviously upset
About something that day
Or had just had enough
Of being mistreated
Or was feeling taken for granted
And decided to bite me
I've been winning that way
For so long now

Saving time
By not actually unlocking
And opening the box
It gives me an indication
Of if there's any mail
Before I spend time unlocking it
But if the mail is further back
In the mailbox tray
I wouldn't know without the key
And if I do feel there is mail
I can't actually get it out anyway
So it's somewhat
An exercise in futility
Somewhat
That day nonetheless
My mailbox decided, not today
We're doing things my way.

NEW HIGH-SPEED DATING

It's for sure
A high-speed, fast-paced
Superhighway
It's because everything is fast
Everybody's moving fast
Now there's no waiting for anything
You can have something at your door
That you order online, the next day
Same day sometimes, for example
It's no different in the dating world
It's like something's there
It gets snapped up straight away
And everyone's looking to be snapped up
So it doesn't hang
There's so much access
You could swipe
One hundred people in one day
Or more
So everything's moving
Fast, fast, fast
People are going on dates
And then
They don't see the person after that

That's how quick
They've decided
That person is not for them
And they're back onto the dating app
The minute they leave that it
Walking out the door of that date
And they're onto the next one
They've already got them lined up
From the one hundred people
That they swiped
So it's all moving very quickly
It's not like back in the day
Where you had to meet someone
And then exchange numbers
And then call
And have that conversation
You're having that
But nowhere near the speed
That it's moving now
People having three dates
In one day
Just because
They've got the technology
To be able to make those dates up
And meet those people
All from different parts

Of whatever city they're in
High-speed, fast-paced
Superhighway
In a good forsaken place
The sad thing about it is
That everybody is moving so fast
That they don't get enough time
To spend with a person
To develop or see
If there's any chemistry
That can be developed or built upon
They're moving so fast
And it's a sad thing
They're not really
Getting to know
Anyone at all enough
And they're often missing something
That could be
Potentially
Worth exploring
It comes with its good and bad.

NEW VEGANS

I feel the vegan food we have now
Marketed and promoted everywhere
As a type of new lifestyle to try out
As some type of healthier option
Is for people that are seeking alternatives
Not for actual non-meat eating vegans
Who detest harming or killing animals
Even though they are the ones
Who probably pushed for more options
In supermarkets, schools, restaurants
I don't think that meat substitute vegan food
Is packaged for those vegans directly
The common question is
Why would vegans want meat substitutes
If they don't want meat
That's because the meat substitutes
Aren't for the devout hardcore vegans
It's not made for them
It's for those other people
Who want to live a healthier lifestyle
Or to feel like they are
Who have now decided

They want to stop eating meat
For whatever reason
They have now decided
Meat is no longer for them
But they still like the taste of meat
They're used to the taste of meat
But they want alternatives
That still taste like it
And are much healthier
Or seemingly much healthier
But that still have and contain
The meat flavour taste that they like
I feel all of these vegan products
Are more aimed at them
People who want to change their lifestyle
And stop eating meat
Who have decided
They're eating healthy now
That actual meat is not good for them
But they still want the taste
I feel all of these no-meat products
Are aimed at them
More so than someone
Raised as a vegan
From a child, for example
Or a hardcore seasoned vegan

Who has been so for a very long time
Who cooks all their own food perhaps
And have never eaten an animal ever
Who wouldn't ever dream it
Who really care about animals
An the environment
Types who really go out and protest
For the rights of those animals
Who are part of animal rights groups
And related organisations
To protect the welfare of animals
And are very passionate about it
People who wouldn't ever consume dairy
Or eat a jelly baby or a wine gum
I don't feel it's at all aimed at them
It couldn't possibly be
It would make no sense
I feel these fancy vegan products
That taste like meat
But aren't meat
Are for people who want to change
From eating meat
And perhaps help the planet
People who are moving
To a healthier diet
To products that some studies say

Are much worse for you
Than eating actual meat
It's marketed to those people
Who would seek it out
As an alternative
To meat products, actual meat
And others who find it trendy
And want to follow
To be alternative, and new
And avant garde
And away from the norm
People who wouldn't care
What milk is used in their coffee
Or what oil their fries are cooked in.

NO PROBLEM

Whenever people
Fail to see your worth
That's their problem
Don't let it be yours.

OF THE TRUEST FORM

A picture has the power
To tell a different story
To each different person
They say, a picture
Paints a thousand words
So you've got a painting
Hanging on the wall
It's telling a story to one person
And it's telling a different story
To the next person
That's a thousand poems to me
A painting
That's one of
The truest forms of poetry
It's poetry that is making itself
It's just poetic
Just to look at a painting
Of whatever that thing is
And the stories
That one image can tell
Is endless
And different
For different people

That's very poetic
To me that's more than poetry
That's more than someone
Sitting down
And writing a poem, to me
And that's very important.

OLD GHOSTS

It would not be
Over charitable
To say
That for all the summers
Missed
Forsaken
You wrote words
That turned into books
Recorded poems
That turned into albums
Filmed thoughts
That turned into a documentary
And in this
You transcended that self
To live in the now
Where the ghosts
Of old wrongs
Cannot abide.

ONE TIME AT RONNIE SCOTT'S

There was a band playing
I was actually part of a film set there
They were filming a movie
Diana
The story of Princess Diana
Played by actress Naomi Watts
So I was there for that
We were filming scenes for that movie
That was my one time
Being at Ronnie Scott's
So it wasn't actually
A real performance, as such
But the band were playing
In the background of the scene
It was all for that
The scene took place at Ronnie Scott's
I haven't seen the film
I don't know if Ronnie Scott's
Was actually in the film as Ronnie Scott's
Or if they were just out
At a random live music place
Or whatever
But Yeah, that was my one time

Going to Ronnie Scott's
I would like to go for an actual night
Where it's not for work
Where it's not just set up
As part of a movie set
Like with a real band playing
Not actors performing
Stopping and starting
When the director says 'cut' and 'action'
Though of course
They were real musicians
But you get the point
I haven't actually been for a night there
A proper night
It was all work really
It's somewhere I'd like to go
For an actual real jazz night
That would be cool
I really do like jazz.

PAIN AND REGRETS

You want to talk to me
But I've left you no option
Than writing messages
We are friends
Before anything
You say
We are human
We make mistakes
Because sometimes
We overthink
That's exactly
What you did
You say
The reason you're suffering
Is due to your own feelings
And overthinking
But that it's not an excuse
You have no right
To hurt my feelings
Or my ego
You say
That there are
Good moments too

To look at
Every minute
Every little thing we did
Comes to your mind
And it's killing you with regrets
And guilt
My silence is hurting you
You want us to communicate
To release our emotions
You say I am a great man
With big and kind heart
That I have no idea
How much it's hurting you
You don't know if I am hurt
Or if am annoyed
With your long messages
And expressions
Or if I'm thinking
You're one crazy woman
Who is not leaving me alone
But you need to know
You need me
To talk to you
To listen to you one more time
So afterwards
We can move on

In a direction we both decide
You say you respect me
That you value me
And that you adore me
That nothing has changed in you
And you're still the same woman
You say all you wish for
Is my hug
And to give me one
But sadly
Your words
Will never
Change what you've done.

PICK OF THE LITTER

She's having a ball
On the dating app
With the number of men
Who have a crush on her
Her ex used to say
That there are more women
On the planet than men
She says it doesn't seem like it here
There are many men who are lonely
Particularly, this one guy
Who is a heart surgeon
As in a cardiologist
Not an emotional healer
Who has a private plane
A yacht
And a mansion to make you melt
Lost his wife and his son
And is now looking for an older woman
To share the rest of his life with
And the wife to share her life with him too
Ideal, ideal, my dear Watson
As Sherlock Holmes would say, she says
But, there's always a 'but'

He lives in Brazil
I have reservation with Brazilian surgeons
It was known in the 60s
That bodies were found
In the street of Rio de Janeiro
Now called Brasilia, she says
And the hearts, lungs
And other expensive organs
Had been removed
To sell on the black market
So, no Brazilian dates for her
And anyway, she said, I don't fly anymore
So it was not meant to be
But her materialistic demon
Was attracted for a moment, not long
So she blocked him
What I like on dating sites, she says
Is the photos men take to be 'at their best'
There's different categories of males
Who think that if they allow
Their dog to lick them all over the face
It will attract the female of their life
Then the old men
With a bush resembling the rain forest
On their chest
Desperately trying to show a six pack

But instead you see a set of protruding ribs
The bloke with his mobile, taking a selfie
I really hate that one, she says
The Chinese man
In his top of the range car
Gold cufflinks and Rolex watch
He should be careful
Not to attract malicious-intentioned villains
He in his profile, introduces himself as
"I am a billionaire in US dollars
Not in the Chinese Yuan currency
I look after you
I love you
You cook for me
And I buy you everything you want"
Wow, who's the dumb woman
Who'll go for him, she says
Then there's the man
Whose photos
Are all about him eating
And eating, and eating
Again, and again
In a transport cafe
And similar outlets
Sitting fifty centimetres
Away from the table

As his belly would lift the table
If he came near it
This site and others
Are really educational
And inspirational, she says
If you are training
To become a psychologist
That's the place to go to and learn
About the colourful male behaviour
To attract his female counterpart
Mind you, she says
The women are not better
Protruding fake boobs in lycra
Ultra mini skirt
No class at all
They're all the same
But I am told, she says
When there is an exception
Meaning herself
She started an emotional earthquake
For she doesn't know what
But nothing like the other uniformists
She feels like an alien
Descending on planet earth
And nobody, not one
Has seen anything like it before

I'm not completely able to tell
If she was being completely serious
Or just completely crazy
As she'd said she's often described
But one thing is completely true
And for myself without doubt
She was indeed
A very unique and special soul.

ROYAL BLACK EGYPTIANS

I've been to Egypt twice
And at both times I went
It was never safe to go
Two weeks before I went
The first time
They had just killed
A group of British tourists there
And it was a big thing in the news
At the time
Everyone was saying
Do not go
That was the general advice
To British holiday makers at that time
And the second time
Two ladies
Where I was going to be staying
Had been eaten by sharks
Right near my resort
And I go in the water
So this was important for me to know
And I saw it
I saw the video footage
Of where it took place

And I realised
That's right where I'm going to be
The water I'd be going into
Is in that stretch
And this woman
She was just having her last dip
Before her journey out of Egypt
And she got eaten by the shark
And I went in that same water
When I got there
Which is crazy to think about
But I did
I'm just crazy like that
So it was never safe
To go at the times I went
And I still went
I don't know
What is safe these days
Yes, you have to consider safety all the time
Anywhere you're going
If there was some kind of unrest
You wouldn't go and throw yourself in it
But I think
The media can blow things up
Way out of proportion
Just for news stories

And speaking about safety
And danger
I definitely felt
For the second time being there
Way better treated
Than I've ever been in London
Both times I went to Egypt
I was treated very well
Everywhere I went
I was never treated less than
Or how I would feel in London
Or in England
Never did I feel that in Egypt
Either time I went
They seem to have a very great respect
For people of colour, for blacks
And it was interesting
Because I saw that whites
Were not treated that way
It was the opposite
It was like the roles reversed when I got
there
And what I understood is
That they have a respect for their history
They know where black people came from
And they know where they come from

They know when the black people arrived
And they know when they arrived
So they have a respect for the history
And it's not necessarily spoken about
But you sense it in the way they treat you
And speak to you
I was also there the second time
With my girlfriend at the time
And the whole male and female thing
Is different there
The man is who is addressed first
In any situation
Whereas in the western world
It's the woman, as in ladies first
That's what's the culture here
Western world culture
Is always ladies first
But it's not that way
In those parts of the world
It's the man's first
The man speaks
The man is addressed
About anything to do with the couple
Whereas here they would ask the lady
They would see her first
Pull out her chair first

Ask her how she's doing
And it's all about the lady
There is very different
It's more about the man
He is the head
It's disrespectful
To speak to the man's woman
And not speak to him
There's a whole different vibe
So that I noticed
On top of the colour thing
Where they treat black people
With a different level of respect
To how they treat white people
And that was a surprise to me
Because I've never experienced that before
To be treated as more important
Pleasantly
It's not what I thought it would be
Or not what I'm used to
So I wouldn't agree with anyone
Who says that they don't treat blacks nicely
I wouldn't say that at all
I felt like royalty on both levels
The fact that I was a male
So obviously the roles reversed

And then also that I was black
So they would pull out my chair first
And not the woman
And my girlfriend at the time was white
So there's that too
So I can't say I agree with that
Bad treatment of blacks
Not not in the parts of Egypt I went to
And I went to many different places as well
My mother was on vacation there recently
And she commented on that very thing too
She noticed the difference in the treatment
As opposed to other people
Who were non black
So that's my experience
And I would go again for that simple reason
It's just nice to be first, for a change
It's nice for someone to see your skin
And just switch up how they treat you
And behave around you
There is a certain respect
It's a switch, you're not ready for
It's like, Oh, wow
This must be what white people feel like
So, yeah, that's my experience
And I treasure it

Don't know if I was just lucky
Don't know if they just liked my face
But that was my experience
My mother confirms it wasn't just me
Because she experienced the same
When she visited
And I will put that down to her being black
And that was her experience
Because she observed
How they were treating others
The same as I did
So, yeah, it's a thing
It's a thing you can look forward to.

SALTED CARAMEL

I will gladly pay
You know why
It's an investment
Today
And the future
And generations to come
Will benefit
I feel it's not going to be
A bad thing
I think
It's going to benefit us
In a big way
The people
And the country
And the planet
That's the one thing
People always have to have
That's not a bad thing
I think there's something good
That can come out of that
I think we're setting ourselves up
For a positive future
These are things

That make the world run
I think it's a grand thing
The sooner the better
It's the way forward, definitely
I think
It's going to improve the world
I think it's going to make
A better tomorrow
It's to make a better world
I really think it's something
That's very much needed
I think it's going to be the resolve
For a lot of things
For a lot of things
We need it
It's the only way forward
For mankind.

SHAVED LEGS AND HIGH HEELS

Years ago
I was appearing on a game show
The contestant and audience
Would basically
Have to guess
Who the real man was
Out of the line up
Of women also on the stage
All with shaved legs
All standing up there in heels
With a cardboard box
Covering their upper half of their body
There were four people altogether
One man and three women
So basically, I had shaved my legs
As I was selected to do the show
And I was up there in heels
With the cardboard box over my head
All you could see is my legs and heels
That's how I quickly learned
What shaving my legs was all about
And how much effort it takes
So I don't envy women

Having to shave their legs often
That once or twice was enough for me
I used a hair removal cream
It was only for television
So it didn't need to razor smooth
To the touch
Only to give the appearance as such
No one was going to be touching my legs
I wasn't going to be rubbing up against anybody
So it didn't matter, even if they were stubbly
Which of course they weren't
In fact after the hair removal
And the application of oily skin lotion
They were glistening smooth
It was all just for the appearance
If I had to razor shave my legs
Or have my legs waxed for it
I think I would have said no altogether
The great thing is though
The airing of it never went ahead
And I'm so glad now looking back
Because I was much younger then
I just did it because I wanted to
It seemed fun at the time

84

And I was breaking into that area of things
Television, and movies, and film
And doing whatever was out there
For me to get involved in
And advance my opportunities
But thankfully they didn't air it in the end
The other interesting thing is
They did film it however
And maybe it still exists out there
somewhere
Much like many of the television
appearances
Movie scenes
Video taped stage performances
And recorded things I've been in
That I've never got to see
I'm just glad now
That particular recording
Didn't make it to television
Maybe it will one day
When I'm on some TV talk show
For something else
Completely unrelated
And they decided dig it out and show it
At least now, years on
I can laugh about it.

SOUL TO THE DEVIL

They say
Whilst you here
You have to feel
You have to love
You have to risk your heart
That you are here
To be swallowed up
Said she took a photo of herself
Minutes after receiving my text
Thank you, she said
For reminding me
Of how special
And beautiful I am
What shall I do, she asked
Do whatever you want, I said
Ask yourself, do you need me
My soul needs you, she whispered
She said, I didn't forget
About any of this
I was just waiting
For the moment when
I'd be ready for you to hear it
I'm afraid of all the things

I wish I could tell you now
All the many things
I've chosen not to
I don't want to be hurt again
Or to be misunderstood
But at the same time
There are things
That I can tell only you
She said, it's hard to choose
Just what to say
When in my mind
I have a whole book
They tell me to write it out
All my thoughts
And create a space
Between me and my mind
But I can't do it, she said
I need a real person to talk to
I'm not a poet, she told them
That I am her book
The one that she shares
Her most intimate thoughts with
Her inner world
I'm the one
Who sees her naked, wounded soul
I can't begin to heal her wounds

So I just listen to her
I just see her
I'm just there
I just listen to her
I'm just the pages in her book
She said if she had right now
Those moments we made love
She would spend all night with me
One of the sacred freedoms
She's now managed to achieve
Since waiting for me
Thinking of me
Wanting me
Whilst trying to forget me
While trying to live without me
While trying to remember
How it was to be with me
They say it's interesting
Your whole story with me
How you haven't stopped dreaming
Since hearing my voice again
They told you
Not to lay down with me
Upon our first time meeting
If you wanted the moment to be more
You asked if I remember then

They tell you I'm very attractive
I'm an artist
That I live in a different world
That I'm one in a million
They say you must be very happy
To have met someone like me
And that they can see
What you've found in me
And I in you
They're curious to see
What will be
You say
I made you feel a woman again
That it's my gift
That I make every woman I am with
Feel special
You say, maybe it is something
That only a poet can do
And that you must be lucky
To have crossed paths with me
You tell me
You would sell your soul
To the devil
To see my eyes again
To kiss me
And you miss me like hell.

TAKE CARE

She thought
I might not talk to her
Ever again
And I almost didn't
She was hurt
Knowing
She may have hurt my feelings
And had not been in peace
A minute since then
She tried to reach me that night
After returning home
Expressing her feelings
Through messages
Saying it's okay
That I might not necessarily
Feel the same way for her
That she totally understands
It's just months we've connected
And that she truly respects that
She was expecting at least
I would say something
Express what's on my heart
Even if only to call her a bitch

Curse her out, and ask her
Who she thought she was
Said she would of loved that
That instead
My quietness killed her
Made her question
All of the time we spent together
That the connection
She felt with me
Was like never before
She hoped maybe
I was the soulmate
That people talk about
She recalled our phone call
From one afternoon
Saying she couldn't really hear
Or understand
Because of the busy train station
And running for the train that day
Said she was so so happy
Over the moon
To get to know me so closely
And wished it to never end
But instead, to have
A meaningful relation with me
That casual dating

Was never her thing
That she's a sensitive person
And a very emotional one
With traumatic experiences
In previous relations she'd had
So she feels the fear
Not knowing exactly how I felt
Didn't know where she was
She was lost with a fear of losing
How naive, she says
And respects
Maybe my silence
Is to be taken as an answer
She'd like to say sorry
A million times
She's missed that peace
The hugs
Terribly
She says that maybe
She's better off alone
So she won't hurt anyone
That she's previous been through
Such pain and darkness
That now she's losing
Every possibility
In trying to run

And escape from there
She wishes me all the luck
Love and laughter
And promises
Not to bother me again
But is there
Any day I want to talk
And give her a chance
To say she's sorry.

THE GIFT OF RESONANCE

I do appreciate
And respect
What comes through me
And comes out of me
Through that communication
With myself and the universe
I appreciate
That I am the chosen for that
Whatever that message
Or word may be
In that particular poem
Or piece of work
I am very appreciative of it
And sometimes
I enjoy sharing in that
Knowing it's helping people
Based on where they are
At a certain time
And knowing
That I'm going to be
Connecting with someone
Because we're always
Somewhere

In the same place
In the universe
At some point
Which is why
People can relate to things
That's where they relate
You know, relativity
Relationship
Connectivity
People can be
On the same page with things
And energy is shared
I don't take that for granted
I appreciate that a lot
And I value that
That what comes through me
Is going to help somebody else
In some way
Or affect them in a way
Whether negatively or positively
It will be a reflection in some way
To move them forward
On their journey
Even if it's just showing them
Where they're at
Just standing still on the spot

They become aware
Of where they are
Because they see something
And something I've said
That resonates with them
I take that to heart
I don't take that very lightly at all
I take that very seriously.

THE RIGHT VIBRATION

Experience has taught me
That when you're dating
You have to find someone
On the same vibrational frequency
What that means is
If you're a person
On a high vibration
And the other person
Is on a lower vibration
What happens is
They will attach themselves to you
Because low always seeks high
They are going find attraction in you
And equally
The majority of high vibrational people
Have the desire to help someone
They are drawn to that need
So you're not always immediately
Going to recognise
At least initially
That their vibration
Is noticeably unequal to
And doesn't match your own
It's important to remain
Conscious of the fact

When your vibration
Doesn't match that persons
And also, that they often
Will disguise themselves
In order to seem as if they do
Experience has taught me well
That you have to date individuals
That reverberate and vibrate
On the same frequency that you do
Because otherwise, what happens is
You'll wake up one day
And suddenly think, hold on a minute
This is not who I am
It's not complimenting my highest purpose
Like, this doesn't feel good for me
I have to get back to me
You'll go your separate ways
And that person
Is going to then
Go and connect with another
Who is more on their frequency
It's more likely to be
Someone that is below
The matching frequency of their own
And then what you need to do
Going forward, is to know this
That others have to match yours
So you can't disclose to people

What it is you want in a partner
You have to let them turn up
Just as they are
Without any prompt from you
Which will allow you
To judge them
Based on just themselves
As they come
Because if you give them
All the templates
And coordinates
Then they'll just show up
And impersonate
The type of person
You said you want
When it's completely not them
So definitely make sure
That you're standing guard
At the door of your frequency
And tell yourself, No
I have to find exactly and organically
Where my frequency is matched
Instead of a person
Who is in need of my frequency
who seeks my high energy
To raise their low vibrational energy up
Because that's the only way it works
Low frequency either comes up to high

Or high has to go down to match low
So which one do you want to do
You need to make the decision
No, I'm standing strong and firm
I know what my boundaries are
I know what my worth is
And I know exactly what I want
These are my requirements
And then you have to go forward
And let that person go off
And match elsewhere
With their low vibrational frequency
Because if you don't
You're going to be dragged down
In a direction that doesn't suit you
And your highest purpose
You'll find yourself caught up
Waking up and saying to yourself
Hold on, this is no longer serving me
And it'll be because
You've done the inner work
If they're not doing that work as well
The necessary inner work to grow
As we're always meant to be growing
And moving and evolving
Then you and that person
Are not going to match
And you're going to notice it

So if you are doing the inner work
Be drawn to a matching
With someone like you
Who is also doing the inside work
On themselves
Who is always in a state of
Self-awareness
And conscious evolution
And elevation
Just make sure
That your eyes are open
And you're doing your homework
And maintaining due diligence
Because we all do it
We all make those mistakes sometimes
Even in our platonic friendships
And within our professional world
Anything where we attach ourselves
To people
To places
And to things
That are no longer serving us
If you're doing the work
Make certain
That you're with someone
Who is equally doing the work
Be reminded of this often
Because we are always

Supposed to be evolving
The work is always incomplete
And will remain so
Until we check out of this place
We continuously supposed to be
Always
Aiming to self-improve
In all aspects of our lives
From the inside out
And the outside in
So make for sure
That you are with someone
Who is vibrationally matched to you
And to your frequency
And if they are not matched
You will start to notice
Different little signs
In that person
These days, we call them 'red flags'
You'll look differently at that person
That's why we often look at our exes
And we're like, damn
What on earth was I thinking
Normally, it's not the way they look
It's often much deeper than that
It's normally their mindset
Choices they've made
Their interests

And then we realise
Oh, that's the reason
Our vibrations
Are on two different frequencies
So go where the energy flows
Without seemingly exhaustive effort
And easily, without friction
Go where you know
You are fulfilling your highest purpose
Otherwise, you're going to look up
To where you know you should be
And you're going to realise
And think to yourself
I've achieved not much
By being in this connection
Instead, I wasted a lot of time.

THE VALUE OF HER SOFTNESS

In a woman
I value sensitivity
Warmth
Femininity
Compassion
Softness
I find often
And no fault of a woman
Often the world and the way it is
In terms of
The way men and women are
Held or projected
In regards to equality
And that kind of thing
Like, man of the house
Male and female roles
I feel like women often have been
And again
Not through any fault of their own
Are kind of forced to take on
This masculine energy
That has for me, when observing
Has reduced the feminine side of them

They're more in their masculine energy
Than their feminine energy as women
And when I talk about softness
I talk about soft and hard
So I look at the masculine
As the hard side
And the feminine, as the soft side
And I find that
Where that masculine energy
Has taken over the feminine energy
It has made them more on the hard side
So the softness is not displayed as much
For whatever reason that has happened
I find I appreciate the softness in a woman
More than the hard
Because it's her natural side
To be that way
Her nature is soft
Her nature is feminine
So I find, sharing space with a woman
We complement each other better that way
When she's in her feminine energy
And I can be my masculine energy
And we're not
Two masculine energies competing
I like that a lot

I appreciate
The softness in the woman a lot
When she's feels free to be able to
Because sometimes
It's because she doesn't feel free
To be in her femininity in its fullness
And most of the time, it's society
And this thing about roles
And this whole gender game
That's probably at the top of my list
I really appreciate a woman's softness
And her femininity
It's sexy
It's like yin and yang
It's like a pull
Push and pull
It draws my energy towards her
The opposite repels it.

THIS MUCH IS SURE

As sure as there's air
Land and water
And a blue sky
I'm telling you now
You won't get anywhere
If you do not try.

THOSE DREAMS AND MORE

Do not let anyone
Ever make you feel
You don't have
What it takes
To achieve
Your dreams
Not ever
Believe
You can
Achieve those
And more.

TONI MORRISON REMINDS US

Art is dangerous
Of the history of artists
Who have been murdered
Slaughtered
Imprisoned
Chopped up
Refused entrance
That the history of art
Whether it's in music
Or written
Or what have you
Has always been bloody
Because dictators
And people in office
And people
Who want to control
And deceive
Know exactly
The people
Who will disturb their plans
And those people
Are artists
They're the ones

That tell the truth
And it's something
That the society
Has got to protect
But when you enter that field
No matter where you are
Whether it's poetry
Or music
Or rather startlingly clear prose
It's a dangerous pursuit
Somebody's out to get you
You have to know it
Before you start
And do it
Under those circumstances
Because it is
One of the most important things
That human beings do.

VERBAL VIOLENCE

Just imagine
All you could accrue
Over time
By learning new words
You never knew
If you developed a vocabulary
You've never ever used
And became offensive
And threatening
And disruptive
And dangerous
And far less innocuous
Much less anodyne
To master the power
Of your vernacular
And get lexical
Like it was sexual
To shroud yourself
In a whole new dialect
Garnering a great new respect
Wherever you went
It's outrageously appalling
To be unprepared

In words
And not comfortably disposed
To attack those foes
With your own well articulated defence
To be verbally canny
And astute with your words
To not be capricious
When the moment requires
But instead, firm and steadfast
And immovable
All the while, still exuding
A carte blanche nature
With effortless exuberance
In the way each word pushes forth
Catalysing new ways of thought
Pulverising pre-conceptions
With your conscientious tongue
Be the contagion
That can't be contained
By the verbiage of others
Converge your words
In such a way
That places your acumen on display
Within all that you say
And reveals the dichotomy
In others supposed intelligence

And the lack of diligence
Pertaining to their own perceptibility
Punctuating their ignorance
Let them then wallow in dysphoria
They deserve it, serves them right
Be lethal in your new enterprise
Take no prisoners, dead or alive
Let not one survive
Be militant and malicious
Very violent and vicious
Spare not any man
Nor any woman
Nor any child
Nor any word
Let them have it
Like a habit
New word for new word
Let it be heard
Go at it like a rabbit
Exhaust them
Until they sound perturbed
And look utterly absurd
Be a savage
It's fundamental
That you galvanise your mental
This, is essential

It is also consequential
That you'll become boldly assertive
But be secretly furtive
Outwitting the wordless
Play all at their own game
Learn this
For it is what you will earn with
And it'll all be worth it
Where the higher hierarchy
Lures the hypergamous
With bared sharp teeth
But you are the greater beast
Cold and dark and prepared to eat
Spare none, don't save them
Bathe them in hypotheticals
Bind them in hysteria
With meticulously placed words
Masked like hidden traps
There's a time to be implicit
This time isn't it
Be sublime with it
Blow their minds with it
Pull the preverbal trigger
Release words with vigour
Provide them no indemnity
Kill them all indefinitely

And intelligently
Indirectly
And indiscriminately
But definitely
Intellectually
Undermining their mandated
Antiquated cadences
And outdated norms
In fine and miraculous form
Refuse to be verbally subdued
Instead be wordy and obtrusive
Even verbally abusive
Salubriously
Be classy and salacious
And ostentatious
Displaying your respect
With a sexy and extensive dialect
Set new parameters
Prove them a slew of amateurs
Simply an obtuse group of animals
Defenceless challengers
Against quick-witted conversation
Idiots falling prey to depredation
Be so good it seems preposterous
That one could be so linguistically refined
Your eloquent use of language

Will retain a place in their minds
Take a firm stance
And simply let the words dance
As they flow and synthesise
While all the rhetoric outside
Is minimised
And your words appear
Emphasised
Unparalleled to every ear
As the world hears them
In wonder and surprise
And you, harmonise.

WHENEVER IT COMES

The awareness side is always there
But it comes in different ways
And just due to habit now
And obviously practice
And through doing it so long
I'm more focused
On how I'm going to capture that moment
I'm always aware that I'm in that moment
And how it has come
And what sparks the inspiration, for
example
Or a thought
Or something I see
Or hear
I'm always aware of that
Because I'm always aware of that naturally
What I focus on now
Is making sure
That I'm in a position
To capture that when it comes
In whatever way it comes
Otherwise, it comes and it goes
And apparently it goes to somebody else

So I always make sure
That since it came to me first
I do what I'm supposed to do with it
The inspiration is floating around
These ideas
This energy
Comes to you
And if you don't harness it
And capture it
And do something with it
It goes off to another person
And they do something with it
It's interesting
I think there's something to that
To a degree
This is my take
From how I have observed myself
And how I look at how my life would be
If it were otherwise
But long story short
My writing
My creative expression
My art
Is all my outlet
It's all my place to put things
To analyse things

To work things out
It's how I manoeuvre through the world
And deal with my pain
And everything
And I realised
Not everybody has that
And I think they don't get to purge
From everything that affects them
So they're just taking it in
Taking it in
Taking it in
I guess they find ways
But they're not always productive ways
And I realise
People are in need of these outlets
And they react
Based on not knowing
Where to put all that energy
Or whatever's going on in their mind
And inside themselves
So they end up crazy
I say that in a kind of jest way
But you know
I think it's important
To have somewhere
To put what the world throws at you

Somewhere to offset it
I think I get to explore myself
And learn things about myself
Through my work
That I wouldn't have explored otherwise
Or had a need to look into
And understand
And pick apart
And some people don't have that capacity
So they manoeuvre through the world
In such a different way
In the way
They handle things
And react to things
And internalise things
And it's a whole different thing
They don't have that processing
So they just
Fly off the handle quite easily
They just carry themselves
Through the world very differently
Another way of looking at it
Is that they manoeuvre themselves
Through others
They don't find a way of analysing
The energies coming through them.

WINNER ANNOUNCED

By the way, she said
You are way better
Than Pessoa
I would say
I found his poems
Difficult to read
But it's hard to say the same
For Bukowski
Because he is really good
He's amazing
But I don't have to choose
Between him and you
I made my choice
A year and a half ago
So, I'll stick to my instincts
And my heart
Bukowski won't write
A poem about me
Bukowski won't call me
At midnight
To ask me how I am
Bukowski won't tell me
How sexy I am

Bukowski won't look
Into my alluring eyes
And tell me
How beautiful they are
Bukowski
Won't make love to me
So, it's a win for you.

WOMEN'S VOLLEYBALL

I like women's volleyball
Because it's beautiful
To watch women
Running around on the beach
In Brazil
In bikinis
Jumping around
That appeals to me
In the sun
On the beach
In bikinis
Jumping around
Playing women's volleyball
It doesn't have to be on the beach
But that's my preference
I could watch women's volleyball anywhere
I would watch it the same way
It would be much more pleasurable
To watch women
Playing women's volleyball
Indoors, even
More so
Than watching sweaty men

Playing football
Running around in shorts
Chasing a ball
Pulling each others shirts
And falling over each other
Women's volleyball
Far more appeals to me
I have no desire to watch men
Running around in shorts
No desire whatsoever
I couldn't tell you about other men
But what I can tell you is about me
They obviously don't dislike it
Otherwise they wouldn't watch it
If they couldn't stand it
They wouldn't watch it
That goes for anyone, for anything
So they're obviously okay with it
They're fine to watch men
Run around in shorts
Even if it's just about the game
That that part doesn't bother them
In any way
And it doesn't bother me
I just have a preference
I absolutely, I would watch women

Running around doing anything
Tennis, one hundred percent
Watching women play Wimbledon
Oh, one hundred percent
Men in shorts, not so much
That would be my choice every time
All jokes aside
I love every sport
But if you gave me a choice
And asked me what sport
I would like enjoy watching most
It would be women's volleyball
Preferably, as said
Beach volleyball
Absolutely
Wow.

THE AUTHOR

Phoenix James is an award winning Writer, Poet, Author and Spoken Word Recording Artist. He began performing his poetic words live on stages across the UK in 1998. His debut spoken word poetry album, The A.R.T.I.S.T, was released in 2000. His first limited edition printed collection of poetry, To Whom It May Concern, was published in 2003. He has toured and performed his poetry internationally since 2004. He has appeared in films, on television and radio shows, and collaborated with other artists, singer-songwriters, actors, musicians, filmmakers and producers. In 2013, he wrote, directed and produced the feature length mock documentary film, Love Freely but Pay for Sex. Phoenix James is the author of several poetry collections and has recorded and released several spoken word poetry albums including Phenzwaan Now & Forever, A Patchwork Remedy for A Broken Melody, FREE, Haven for the Tormented, With All That Said, Light Beams from the Void, The Love So Far, and over seventy spoken word poetry singles. All are available online now and streaming everywhere worldwide.

If you enjoyed reading this book, please leave a review or comment online. The author reads every review and they help new readers discover and experience his amazing work.

PHOENIX JAMES

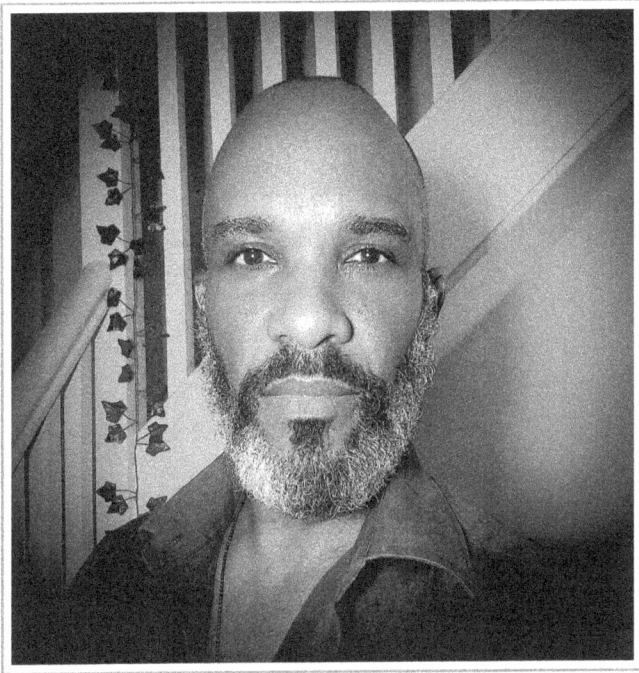

Photo by Phoenix James

Phoenix James lives in London, England.

Connect with Phoenix James online via his social media platforms and let others know that you've been fortunate to discover this book. To contact or learn more about Phoenix James and his creative journey or to receive updates via his Newsletter Mailing List, visit his official website at www.PhoenixJamesOfficial.com

Phoenix James Official